CROSS-CULTURAL ESSENTIALS 4

COMMUNICATION AND CULTURE

AN IN-DEPTH EXPLORATION OF CULTURE AND COMMUNICATION

21 TUTORIALS WITH DISCUSSION
POINTS AND ACTIVITIES

Communication and Culture
An in-depth exploration of culture and communication
Communication Foundations, Module 4 of the Cross-Cultural Essentials Curriculum

Copyright © 2019, 2016 AccessTruth

Version 1.2

ISBN: 978-0-9944270-5-2

All Rights Reserved. Except as may be permitted by the Copyright Act, no part of this publication may be reproduced in any form or by any means without prior permission from the publisher. Requests for permission should be made to info@accesstruth.com

Unless otherwise indicated, all Scripture quotations are taken from the Holy Bible, New Living Translation, copyright © 1996, 2004. Used by permission of Tyndale House Publishers, Inc., Wheaton, Illinois 60189. All rights reserved.

Published by AccessTruth
PO Box 8087
Baulkham Hills NSW 2153
Australia

Email: info@accesstruth.com
Web: accesstruth.com

Cover and design by Matthew Hillier
Edited by Simon Glover

Table of Contents

About the Cross-Cultural Essentials Curriculum 5

TUTORIAL 4.1 7
God has spoken 1

TUTORIAL 4.2 15
God has spoken 2

TUTORIAL 4.3 21
The Treasure

TUTORIAL 4.4 27
Keep, guard, entrust

TUTORIAL 4.5 33
What is culture?

TUTORIAL 4.6 41
Understanding culture

TUTORIAL 4.7 49
The concept of self

TUTORIAL 4.8 55
Discovering your own culture

TUTORIAL 4.9 65
Personal vs. societal obligations

TUTORIAL 4.10 71
Styles of communication 1

TUTORIAL 4.11 79
Styles of communication 2

TUTORIAL 4.12 89
The concept of time

TUTORIAL 4.13 95
Culture in the workplace

TUTORIAL 4.14 107
Control: Who is in charge?

TUTORIAL 4.15 113
Social relationships

TUTORIAL 4.16 121
Culture/Language acquisition 1

TUTORIAL 4.17 137
Culture/Language acquisition 2

TUTORIAL 4.18 151
Becoming a communicator 1

TUTORIAL 4.19 159
Becoming a communicator 2

TUTORIAL 4.20 167
Practical communication 1

TUTORIAL 4.21 175
Practical communication 2

About the Cross-Cultural Essentials Curriculum

It's no secret that there are still millions of people in the world living in "unreached" or "least-reached" areas. If you look at the maps, the stats, and the lists of people group names, it's almost overwhelming. The people represented by those numbers can't find out about God, or who Jesus Christ is, or what He did for them because there's no Bible in their language or church in their area – they have *no access* to Truth.

So you could pack a suitcase and jump on a plane, but then what? How would you spend your first day? How would you start learning language? When would you tell them about Jesus? Where would you start? The truth is that a mature, grounded fellowship of God's children doesn't just "happen" in an unreached area or even in your neighborhood. When we speak the Truth, we need to have the confidence that it is still the same Truth when it gets through our hearer's language, culture and worldview grid.

The *Cross-Cultural Essentials* curriculum, made up of 10 individual modules, forms a comprehensive cross-cultural training course. Its main goal is to help equip believers to be effective in providing people access to God's Truth through evangelism and discipleship. The *Cross-Cultural Essentials* curriculum makes it easy to be better equipped for teaching the whole narrative of the Bible, for learning about culture and worldview and for planting a church and seeing it grow.

More information on the curriculum can be found at *accesstruth.com*

Introduction to Module 4: Communication and Culture

Module 4 begins by focusing on God's desire to communicate clearly, and what it is that He wants to communicate. All human communication takes place within the context of culture, so Module 4 is an in-depth exploration of culture; what it is, and how we can understand it. Understanding our own culture more objectively begins by making comparisons between different cultures in specific areas, such as the concept of time, areas of obligation, styles of communication, and social relationships. Module 4 finishes by giving an introduction to the major principles of acquiring another language and culture and becoming a clear communicator in another culture.

ABOUT THE CROSS-CULTURAL ESSENTIALS CURRICULUM

How to use this module

 Read / watch / listen: Read through the tutorial. If you have an online account at *accesstruth.com*, or the DVD associated with this module you can watch the video or listen to the audio of the tutorial.

 Discussion Points: At the end of some tutorials there are discussion points. It may be helpful to write down your answers so you can process your thoughts. If you are doing the tutorials in a group, these points should prove helpful in guiding the discussion.

 Activities: Some tutorials have activities that involve practical tasks, worksheets that need to be completed, or may just ask for a written answer.

Primary Contributors

Paul and Linda Mac spent 11 years in Papua New Guinea involved in pioneering church planting in an isolated people group. They were privileged to see God plant a number of churches in that area that continue to thrive today. During the time there, they headed up a translation team that produced a New Testament in the local language. After leaving PNG, Paul and Linda worked for 12 years in leadership and consultative roles with an international mission agency. Today they continue to provide church planting guidance for a number of different teams engaged in some of the world's most challenging contexts. They are passionate about seeing churches planted that are well equipped to carry on for future generations.

4.1 God has spoken 1

OBJECTIVES OF THIS TUTORIAL

This tutorial introduces the whole area of *communication* by looking at God as the *Great Communicator*. It focuses on God's actions in history to show that communication is an inherent feature of His character and that He always desires to communicate clearly and effectively.
It also introduces the idea that God has chosen to use human beings to communicate His message to Man.

God gives meaning to communication

> **JOHN 1:1** In the beginning the Word already existed. The Word was with God, and the Word was God.

God always shows His personality in communication - just like holiness or love, communication is inherent in the character of God.

That anything can (1) truly be known, and (2) that it can actually be spoken about, is rooted in the nature of God, because He is the original Communicator. Without a personal God, no idea or word has greater value than another. There is no sound in a vacuum, and no real communication without God.

God communicates through creation

Creation was an act of communication - into the great silence of eternity, He spoke - "Let there be light".

> **PSALM 33:6** The LORD merely spoke, and the heavens were created. He breathed the word, and all the stars were born.

> **ROMANS 1:20** For ever since the world was created, people have seen the earth and sky. Through everything God made, they can clearly see his invisible qualities—his eternal power and divine nature. So they have no excuse for not knowing God.

God made man to listen

GENESIS 1:27 So God created human beings in his own image.

God made man to hear Him - with a mind and emotions and a will - so that we have the ability to understand and love and choose to obey our Creator. The One who speaks and communicates created people who could hear and understand Him. As we come to teach His Word we can have this assurance about the people we teach.

God speaks with man

Having made someone to listen, God always speaks to him -

"And God said..." "God said to the man..." "And the Lord commanded the man..."

God has never left man in a moral limbo. Man's life was to be a response to the ongoing revelation of who God is. Understanding and a real knowledge of God would result in love, worship and obedience.

GENESIS 3:9 Then the LORD God called to the man, "Where are you?"

He is not just a distant God passing on divine laws, but a personal God, involved in the lives and everyday affairs of human beings.

Sin breaks communication

Adam and Eve listened to God's Enemy.

GENESIS 3:5 "God knows that your eyes will be opened as soon as you eat it, and you will be like God, knowing both good and evil."

They chose to be speakers rather than listeners - to tell their own story rather than to hear God tell it from his own, true, perspective. Then shame and fear entered into the relationship for the first time. Communication was broken.

God's gracious commitment to communication is unfailing

Even at that point God promised the coming of the One who would restore communication fully.

Down through the years, God was the one who maintained communication. He sought to communicate through His chosen people. Through the prophets. He lived among them in a house made of the skins of animals. He provided the means of the sacrifices as a temporary covering for sins.

Even though they refused to listen many times, He did not stop speaking. Through angels, on stone tablets, on a wall, in dreams, through unbelievers, even through a donkey... in a small still voice and in thunder - God showed His grace and His desire to communicate.

> **NEHEMIAH 9:17,30,31** They refused to obey and did not remember the miracles you had done for them... [30] In your love, you were patient with them for many years. You sent your Spirit, who warned them through the prophets. But still they wouldn't listen! So once again you allowed the peoples of the land to conquer them. [31] But in your great mercy, you did not destroy them completely or abandon them forever. What a gracious and merciful God you are!

God communicated Himself through Christ

> **ISAIAH 7:14** All right then, the Lord himself will give you the sign. Look! The virgin will conceive a child! She will give birth to a son and will call him Immanuel (which means 'God is with us').

> **JOHN 1:9** The one who is the true light, who gives light to everyone, was coming into the world.

> **JOHN 1:14** So the Word became human and made his home among us. He was full of unfailing love and faithfulness. And we have seen his glory, the glory of the Father's one and only Son.

> **HEBREWS 1:1** Long ago God spoke many times and in many ways to our ancestors through the prophets. [2] And now in these final days, he has spoken to us through his Son. God promised everything to the Son as an inheritance, and through the Son he created the universe. [3] The Son radiates God's own glory and expresses the very character of God, and he sustains everything by the mighty power of his command. When he had cleansed us from our sins, he sat down in the place of honor at the right hand of the majestic God in heaven.

God restored communication at Calvary

> **MATTHEW 27:50,51** Then Jesus shouted out again, and he released his spirit. [51] At that moment the curtain in the sanctuary of the Temple was torn in two, from top to bottom. The earth shook, rocks split apart.

HEBREWS 10:19,20 And so, dear brothers and sisters, we can boldly enter heaven's Most Holy Place because of the blood of Jesus. [20] By his death, Jesus opened a new and life-giving way through the curtain into the Most Holy Place.

EPHESIANS 2:18 Now all of us can come to the Father through the same Holy Spirit because of what Christ has done for us.

God speaks to His children by His Spirit who lives in them

JOHN 16:13 When the Spirit of truth comes, he will guide you into all truth. He will not speak on his own but will tell you what he has heard. He will tell you about the future.

ROMANS 8:14 For all who are led by the Spirit of God are children of God.

The Holy Spirit will communicate through us and guide us as we communicate with others.

God speaks through His word

ROMANS 10:17 So faith comes from hearing, that is, hearing the Good News about Christ.

2 TIMOTHY 3:16,17 All Scripture is inspired by God and is useful to teach us what is true and to make us realize what is wrong in our lives. It corrects us when we are wrong and teaches us to do what is right.[17] God uses it to prepare and equip his people to do every good work.

From God's mercy and grace (His "condescension" - no adequate word in our lexicon), He chooses to partner with man in communicating His will - His, the Creator's, version of the way things actually are, and the way they should be.

He appointed man (the beings created in His image) as His ambassadors - His mouthpieces to the rest of creation. He chose man to communicate. His Word - God breathed, written by human hand, spoken by the prophets, in human languages, into fallen human cultures, using human devices of communication: idiom, analogies, metaphors, parables.

The ultimate proof of God's commitment to speaking with a human voice, in a way that is intelligible to man, is the incarnation.

1 JOHN 1:1 We proclaim to you the one who existed from the beginning, whom we have heard and seen. We saw him with our own eyes and touched him with our own hands. He is the Word of life.

The pre-existent God, the Creator, now communicating with a human voice, with human gestures, through visible actions and reactions - Truth was personified in human form.

> **1 JOHN 1:2-3** This one who is life itself was revealed to us, and we have seen him. And now we testify and proclaim to you that he is the one who is eternal life. He was with the Father, and then he was revealed to us. ³ We proclaim to you what we ourselves have actually seen and heard so that you may have fellowship with us. And our fellowship is with the Father and with his Son, Jesus Christ.

And the incarnation gives us the message, mandate and model to be teachers, proclaimers, disciplers, modelers of Truth likewise. And to call others into this same privilege - to be God's mouthpiece and embodiment for Truth.

God speaks through His church

> **MARK 3:14** Then he appointed twelve of them and called them his apostles. They were to accompany him, and he would send them out to preach.

> **ACTS 1:8** But you will receive power when the Holy Spirit comes upon you. And you will be my witnesses, telling people about me everywhere - in Jerusalem, throughout Judea, in Samaria, and to the ends of the earth.

> **EPHESIANS 3:10** God's purpose in all this was to use the church to display his wisdom in its rich variety to all the unseen rulers and authorities in the heavenly places.

We (the Church) are God's first choice for communicating His Truth. On the day of Pentecost, as the plan of God for His church was becoming clearer, Peter spoke to the people who were gathered there from many different countries.

> **ACTS 2:39** "This promise is to you, and to your children, and even to the Gentiles— all who have been called by the Lord our God."

> **1 CHRONICLES 16:24** Publish his glorious deeds among the nations. Tell everyone about the amazing things he does.

GOD HAS SPOKEN 1

❓ DISCUSSION POINTS

1. Think about the specific ways God's Enemy has attempted to divert man's attention from God's clear message through Creation. How has he tried to confuse what God is saying through creation, and what effect has that had on the ways people see the world around them?

2. Hebrews 1:1 says, *"Long ago God spoke many times and in many ways to our ancestors through the prophets."* What are some of the specific ways and times that God communicated with man before the coming of His Son?

➡ ACTIVITIES

1. Read the following short write-up on four elements of effective communication. As you have conversations with people this week, make sure to actively think about these aspects of communication. Make some notes summarizing your observations:

- Do you agree that these four aspects are important, and can you think of any more areas to add?
- How effective are you in applying these things as you communicate?
- How effective were the people you spoke to in clearly communicating? (you don't have to mention any names…)
- Can you relate any of these aspects to the way God communicates?

Four Elements of Effective Communication

Be concise - Don't say more than you have to say to get your message across clearly. It's important to try to be clear and unambiguous when you communicate with others. Taking a long time to say something can be frustrating for your listeners and can even obscure your main message.

Be a good listener - You need to listen to the person you are trying to communicate with. Why? Because your message must be heard for good communication to take place. People will not listen to you if your message isn't relevant to them. You will not be relevant if you have not engaged with who the other person is, and what they are saying. They have no obligation to listen to you if you have shown no interest in listening to them. So, one of the most important communication skills to have is to be a good, active listener. If you tune someone out or already know what you're going to say when he stops talking, you're not listening. Most people just want to be heard.

Ask for Feedback - Make sure that you get your message across to the other person by asking for feedback. Listen to the person's response, and respond with anything that didn't come across clearly. You can avoid a lot of miscommunication by going one step further and asking the other person for their opinion on a topic or for their reaction to your ideas.

Non-verbal Communication - Non-verbal communication is just as important as verbal communication, and people are very good at reading what you are really thinking. Facial expressions, body language and tone of voice all convey important information about how you feel about what you are saying. How you say something can completely change how your actual words are received.

4.2 God has spoken 2

OBJECTIVES OF THIS TUTORIAL

This tutorial continues to introduce the whole area of communication by focusing on God's communication with Man. God's reasons for communicating and the content of His communication are also discussed here, as well as what His communication reveals about His character.

So what is God saying?

Anyone who is willing to look can see God's creation around them. And they can see God's character - power and majesty - reflected there.

> **ROMANS 1:20** For ever since the world was created, people have seen the earth and sky. Through everything God made, they can clearly see his invisible qualities—his eternal power and divine nature. So they have no excuse for not knowing God.

But 1 Chronicles 16:24 and Psalm 66 tell us that God wants people to know the things He has done.

> **PSALM 66:1-5** Shout joyful praises to God, all the earth! ² Sing about the glory of his name! Tell the world how glorious he is. ³ Say to God, "How awesome are your deeds! Your enemies cringe before your mighty power. ⁴ Everything on earth will worship you; they will sing your praises, shouting your name in glorious songs." Interlude ⁵ Come and see what our God has done, what awesome miracles he performs for people!

God has told us what He is doing

God is at work and always has been. He is not the distant God of Islam nor is He the impersonal force of Buddhism. He acts in the affairs of humans. Since the dawn of history, God has been at work in the world - it is the stage on which God has chosen to act.

> **JOHN 5:17** But Jesus replied, "My Father is always working, and so am I."

The Lord Jesus had this overwhelming sense of God at work and of Himself working within God's plan. The rest of the universe is filled with angelic and human spectators, watching what God is doing.

History is about God's Work, and Scripture is God's account of that Work. It is God telling His Story. He calls all men to know about His works and His work.

God has the leading role in His Story

> **PSALM 66:5** Come and see what our God has done, what awesome miracles he performs for people!

We should see with eyes which observe His work, from the beginning. To understand what He has done "from the beginning" and to know what He is doing now, and what He plans to do until time and history are completed.

The Bible is God's account of His work - past, present and future. Too often the Church has mistakenly seen the Bible as "the stories of people and their encounters with God" - rather than God's story of His work and His planned encounters with man.

God has the Leading Role in the whole drama of redemption - and the Bible is God's record of His work throughout the history of the world.

> **1 CHRONICLES 16:24-29** Publish his glorious deeds among the nations. Tell everyone about the amazing things he does. [25] Great is the LORD! He is most worthy of praise! He is to be feared above all gods. [26] The gods of other nations are mere idols, but the LORD made the heavens! [27] Honor and majesty surround him; strength and joy fill his dwelling. [28] O nations of the world, recognise the LORD, recognise that the LORD is glorious and strong. [29] Give to the LORD the glory he deserves! Bring your offering and come into his presence. Worship the LORD in all his holy splendor.

The theme of God's Story is His Glory

So God has told His story, the story of His deeds, His work - what He has done, is doing and will do - and the central theme is His Glory. The Bible is God's revelation of His Glory.

Beginning with His creation of the world and continuing step by step through history, God has demonstrated the wonders of His own glorious person. This is the focus of His communication. He could not withhold this from us because to do so would be less than loving, less than gracious, less than righteous.

What God has done and said

Most Christians generally consider the Scriptures to be the record of the words of God - what He has said. We often fail to see God's Word also as His account to the world of His deeds, His actions - what He has done. God has revealed himself as He walked through history with men.

How God has shared His Story

As we said - God, the Communicator, the Teacher, created man to understand. God fully comprehends the human mind. He knows the best way to communicate with that mind, and God has chosen the best form to communicate His Story.

Who He is - revealed through His actions

He revealed Himself to Israel

The things God recorded in the Scriptures actually happened in time and space. He spoke, He acted, and interacted with real people - people just like us.

He reminded Israel of His true identity and pointed them back to His historical relationships.

> **EXODUS 3:15** God also said to Moses, "Say this to the people of Israel: Yahweh, the God of your ancestors - the God of Abraham, the God of Isaac, and the God of Jacob - has sent me to you. This is my eternal name, my name to remember for all generations.

God said to the Children of Israel - if you want to know who I am, remember how I acted in relationships with your fathers.

Remember Egypt, the Passover, the wilderness.

Did my promises fail? I allowed judgment to fall on you, because of your idolatry and disobedience, but I was faithful to deliver you.

> **DEUTERONOMY 7:18,19** Just remember what the LORD your God did to Pharaoh and to all the land of Egypt.[19] Remember the great terrors the LORD your God sent against them. You saw it all with your own eyes! And remember the miraculous signs and wonders, and the strong hand and powerful arm with which he brought you out of Egypt. The LORD your God will use this same power against all the people you fear.

God revealed Himself in history. Their leaders and prophets constantly reminded Israel of that history. Their faith rested on God as He revealed Himself through His historical acts. God's story of who He is, revealed through His actions, was the basis for the faith of each successive generation.

Individuals had to exercise personal faith - but not faith in a subjective experience. They had to exercise faith in God, the redeemer of their nation, as He had acted clearly in history.

He revealed Himself in Christ

God's ultimate revelation was through Christ.

God stepped into the pages of history and acted in the form of a human - God in action - God walking the roads of Palestine, showing His power over the elements, over Satan, sin and death - and interacting with people.

When Philip said "Lord, show us the Father", (John 14:9) Jesus replied, "Have I been with you all this time, Philip, and yet you still don't know who I am? Anyone who has seen me has seen the Father! So why are you asking me to show him to you?"

This too is God telling His Story.

The Apostles' Story

The Apostles saw the Old Testament as God's record of what He had been doing in the world - especially with His chosen people. The Old Testament was the Bible of the early church.

The Apostles' teaching as recorded in Acts emphasized God's historical actions as He related to Abraham, Isaac, Jacob, Joseph, Moses and David. They then showed the links between those acts of God in the Old Testament with His revelation of Himself in the Story of His Son - Jesus Christ of Nazareth.

The Apostles interpreted the whole of Christ's coming, His birth, death, resurrection, present glory and all future revelations of His majesty on the basis of the accounts and prophecies of the Old Testament. They used the Old Testament to authenticate the claim of Jesus of Nazareth to be the Christ, the Anointed One.

For them, His Story began long before they met Him beside the Sea of Galilee or the River Jordan - what they saw of His life fitted with what they already knew of God as revealed through His actions. They taught the Old Testament and its history along with the events they had just experienced with Jesus of Nazareth as One Story.

Our responsibility to tell the whole Story

We have thought about the fact that God communicates, and that He created man so that he could communicate with Him - to reveal His glory. Sin has created obstacles to that but God has continued to speak. He has given us the Story of His actions in space and time - how He has acted (worked) - to deal with sin and death and Satan.

That is the Story that has been entrusted to the Church. To us. He wants us to tell the whole Story. To recount His true account of History. He wants us to communicate fully and clearly as He Himself has.

? DISCUSSION POINTS

1. The tutorial states that *"most Christians generally consider the Scriptures to be the record of the words of God - what He has said. We often fail to see God's Word also as His account to the world of His deeds, His actions - what He has done."* Would you agree with this statement? Does it reflect the general view or teaching of the Christian community you are most familiar with? Explain why you think their view has formed in the way it has.

2. It has been said by some people that God has not clearly revealed Himself and is 'hidden', so that therefore His judgment of people is not fair. What would you say to someone who presented that view to you?

ACTIVITIES

1. Find two quotes from the Apostles that show clearly their level of personal commitment to telling God's story.

4.3 The Treasure

OBJECTIVES OF THIS TUTORIAL

This tutorial continues to build the Biblical foundation for clear communication. It focuses on the nature of God's Word - the Written Word and the Living Word.

God graciously gave His word to the nation of Israel

Not only is God holy, just and loving, but He also communicates His character and His will. He has always spoken to man and is committed to communicating - no matter how rebellious and indifferent men are. After sin entered and communication was broken, God promised the One who would restore things. He also provided a temporary way for men to come to Him - through sacrifices. He also raised up a nation, His own chosen people, and they were to be the line through which the promised One would come.

> **GENESIS 26:4** I will cause your descendants to become as numerous as the stars of the sky, and I will give them all these lands. And through your descendants all the nations of the earth will be blessed.

They would also be the means by which God would preserve a treasure given - His written Word. He did this despite the many times they were disobedient and turned away from Him. God's unwavering commitment to speaking with man is only because of His grace. There is nothing we can do to earn this incredible gift.

Pride, unbelief and rebellion kept Israel from communicating God's Word to the world

God's intention was for His people to see His Word as a treasure that they should obey and preserve. He gave them the task of taking the Truth about Him, the One True God, to others who did not know Him. They were to do this by being an example in the way they lived so that others would be drawn to Him. They would then teach those people the Truth contained in His Word, and so in this way, God would speak to all men, no matter what their language or where they came from.

> **ISAIAH 49:6** He says, "You will do more than restore the people of Israel to me. I will make you a light to the Gentiles, and you will bring my salvation to the ends of the earth."

Down through history, this did happen sometimes. Other people did come and were taught the truth. But more often than not, God's people, the Jews, failed in the Task God had given them.

They were proud of the fact that they had been entrusted with God's Word. But rather than treasuring it as His gracious communication to them and all men, they spent their efforts trying to follow every word. They thought they could do so in their own strength, but in truth they had no hope of pleasing God themselves. Sometimes, weary of this fruitless effort, they ignored His Law entirely for years at a time.

Under the New Covenant, a new group of messengers was chosen

That was the old agreement, or covenant. With the coming of the living Word, and then through His death and resurrection, God brought about a new covenant. Now God's grace was fully revealed, not only for salvation from sin, but also in how His children could live lives pleasing to Him.

To give His children the strength to live, He sent His Spirit to be here and live in them. At the time when God's Spirit came, He gave special ability to certain people who wrote down His revelation to them. They told the story of the living Word. The story of the beginnings of the church, God's chosen people under the new agreement, was also written. They told how God spoke through His people to the Jews and also other people. And letters were written - to real people in real situations. Instructions from God for how individuals and groups of His children should live. And God's Spirit gave glimpses of the future, as an encouragement for the church to wait for the return of the Master.

The Old Testament is part of the Church's treasure

The New Covenant replaced the Old, but God's original revelation to the Jews still has a place. It contains the story of God's actions in history. It records the fall of Lucifer, the mighty angel who became God's Enemy; it tells how sin entered the world, it records the promises about the Messiah, and it also records God's law, His perfect standards that remain unchanged. Christ repeatedly quoted from the Old Testament and the early church treasured it as God's Word.

> **1 CORINTHIANS 10:11** These things happened to them as examples for us. They were written down to warn us who live at the end of the age.

The New Testament reveals what was left hidden

The Old can only be fully understood in light of the New. In the Old much was still hidden, many mysteries still existed, even for those to whom God gave special knowledge - His prophets. Christ revealed some, but much of what He spoke was in parables and spoken in pictures.

> **MATTHEW 13:35** This fulfilled what God had spoken through the prophet: "I will speak to you in parables. I will explain things hidden since the creation of the world."

But most could not be fully revealed until the Holy Spirit came into the world to be with the Church and live in God's children.

> **JOHN 16:12,13** "There is so much more I want to tell you, but you can't bear it now. [13] When the Spirit of truth comes, he will guide you into all truth. He will not speak on his own but will tell you what he has heard. He will tell you about the future".

As in the Old Testament, God's Spirit chose men - the Apostles - prophets of the New Testament, to whom He revealed Truth, which they wrote down. The many mysteries left from the Old Testament were made clear. God's plan was revealed - a new group had been chosen. Not based on ancestry or race or language, but chosen in Christ. Those who believed His Word saw themselves as sinners and accepted Christ's sacrifice as the payment for their sins.

> **EPHESIANS 3:4-6** As you read what I have written, you will understand my insight into this plan regarding Christ. [5] God did not reveal it to previous generations, but now by his Spirit he has revealed it to his holy apostles and prophets. [6] And this is God's plan: Both Gentiles and Jews who believe the Good News share equally in the riches inherited by God's children. Both are part of the same body, and both enjoy the promise of blessings because they belong to Christ Jesus.

We, the Church, are the means God chooses to pass on the Treasure

Just as God committed the older part of the treasure to the nation of Israel, now He has committed the completed treasure to the Church. And just as it was His desire that others, still in darkness, be drawn to the light, so it is for us.

The living Word has gone back to the Father. His Church is now His body, His presence, on the earth. We are now God's communication to the World, by our lives and through our message. We have the complete Treasure. We know the Living Word, we have His Written Word, and we have the Spirit of Truth living in us. We have all that is needed for a man to live as God would have him to live.

> **2 PETER 1:3** By his divine power, God has given us everything we need for living a godly life. We have received all of this by coming to know him, the one who called us to himself by means of his marvelous glory and excellence.

We are rich. The question is, what will we do with our riches, with this treasure? He was rich but became poor for us. Will we do the same for others?

> **2 CORINTHIANS 8:9** You know the generous grace of our Lord Jesus Christ. Though he was rich, yet for your sakes he became poor, so that by his poverty he could make you rich.

God enables us to be His messengers

We are weak and lacking in wisdom. But we are what God has chosen to contain the treasure, and to give it out so that others can also know and speak with the living God as their Father.

> **2 CORINTHIANS 4:3-7** If the Good News we preach is hidden behind a veil, it is hidden only from people who are perishing. ⁴ Satan, who is the god of this world, has blinded the minds of those who don't believe. They are unable to see the glorious light of the Good News. They don't understand this message about the glory of Christ, who is the exact likeness of God. ⁵ You see, we don't go around preaching about ourselves. We preach that Jesus Christ is Lord, and we ourselves are your servants for Jesus' sake. ⁶ For God, who said, "Let there be light in the darkness," has made this light shine in our hearts so we could know the glory of God that is seen in the face of Jesus Christ. ⁷ We now have this light shining in our hearts, but we ourselves are like fragile clay jars containing this great treasure. This makes it clear that our great power is from God, not from ourselves.

❓ DISCUSSION POINTS

1. How do you think the Church today understands its role in passing on the Treasure? Is it seen as being a responsibility for just some people within the church, or something that each believer should be involved in? Give examples from your own experience.

2. What would you say is the view of unbelievers in your country/community of the Bible (in general culture)? Can you think of examples of how that view is reflected in the media?

➡ ACTIVITIES

1. Talk to two believers that you know about God's Word and find out the following:
- What role does God's Word play in their everyday life?
- Ask them to imagine a believer in another country who doesn't have the Bible in a language they can read - in what ways do they think that person might be effected?

2. Reflect on what it would be like if you did not have access to God's Word in your own language.

3. Search for and watch videos online that show people receiving God's Word translated into their own language for the first time, e.g. 'Treasuring God's Word', showing the Kimyal Tribe in Papua, Indonesia receiving the New Testament in their own language.

4.4 Keep, guard, entrust

OBJECTIVES OF THIS TUTORIAL

This tutorial discusses the idea that we are to make the Truth part of our own lives, see that it is not changed or lost, and then pass it on to others.

God completes perfectly everything He sets out to do

One of the characteristics of God that we see many times is that what He does, He does well. After each step of creation He said that it was good. Many of the things we do, we have to plan as we go, but God sees the end from the beginning and so always completes what He sets about doing. Nothing takes Him by surprise.

The plan of salvation - how He would bring men back into communication with Himself - is a complete plan, with nothing left out. Each of the prophecies about the coming of the Messiah proved to be correct. The pictures and signs were all accurate to the last detail. And then when He came, Christ, the living Word, said and did all that the Father asked of Him.

> **JOHN 17:4,8** I brought glory to you here on earth by completing the work you gave me to do... ⁸ for I have passed on to them the message you gave me. They accepted it and know that I came from you, and they believe you sent me.

His plan for the church too is a perfect one. Although we do not always see each part of what He has done, is doing and will do - we can be confident that it will be as he wants it to be. He said that Satan and all the forces of hell can't stop His church being built.

His plan for individual believers is also perfect and complete. He made a way for them to be redeemed (bought back) and washed through His blood, and for them to live in victory over sin, through His resurrection. And his plans for how we will live with Him forever, those will also come about - exactly as He plans.

> **EPHESIANS 4:12,13** Their responsibility is to equip God's people to do his work and build up the church, the body of Christ. ¹³ This will continue until we all come to such

unity in our faith and knowledge of God's Son that we will be mature in the Lord, measuring up to the full and complete standard of Christ.

God's Word is one entire body of truth and needs to be passed on intact

The treasure - God's Word - as we have said, is also complete. Through his Spirit, He has given us all we need to know - to be born again, to worship Him as our Father, and to live as His mature sons and daughters.

All too often, God's children have not really understood this. They have not treasured all of God's Word. They have not seen it as complete and perfect or been committed to understanding and protecting and passing on the Whole Truth which has been given to us.

Rather than seeing God's Word as a whole, with each part providing a balance, too often they only concentrate on certain sections. Or they chop it up, looking at small parts separate from the whole, never seeing it as one story, one letter from God to man, one body of truth.

Still others feel they have to come up with new and exciting programs - original ways of packaging truth. Many times the basis for these are the felt needs or desires of people.

Some are only concerned with telling people what they need to know to be saved. Rather than carefully laying foundations so that people see their need for salvation, they present the answer before hearts are prepared.

Many too are not committed to teaching all that the new believer needs to know of the truth so they can live as God wants them to. This is like a mother giving birth to a child and then leaving it to look after itself.

Fear can keep us from a commitment to passing on the treasure intact, but God's Spirit gives us all that we need

In 2 Timothy, Paul the apostle writes to his young trainee, Timothy. Paul has been sentenced to death, and this, we understand, is his last letter - written from a Roman dungeon. In the first few verses Paul reminds this young man that it was God's Spirit Himself who gave Timothy the ability to do the task which Paul had been training him to do. And he says:

> **2 TIMOTHY 1:7** For God has not given us a spirit of fear and timidity, but of power, love, and self-discipline.

For Timothy to do the task that Paul is now handing over to him, he will not be able to be fearful. Sometimes it is fear that keeps us from committing ourselves to the task of teaching God's Word in its entirety: "What if my knowledge is lacking? What if people are not happy with it? What if they reject the truth, or I'm not able to take on this task?"

But Paul told Timothy that thoughts like that do not come from God. His Spirit gives us, first of all, power. What is this power? It is God's Word itself. As we faithfully teach and pass on God's Word, He takes it, makes it come alive in people's hearts and produces change in their lives.

But people are not always responsive to our teaching. They don't always appreciate what we are passing on to them. We can become fearful of wasting our time, of not being liked. But as Paul reminded Timothy, it is God's Spirit who produces love in our hearts for those we are to teach. We cannot love them sufficiently, but He can give us Christ's love for them.

Sometimes it is fear of our own failure that keeps us from committing to such a huge task. What if I can't keep up with the study and preparation? What if I say I'm going to do it but then fail? Again, it is God's Spirit living in us that can give us the clear minds and disciplined lives that are required.

We are to make the Truth part of our own lives, see that it is not changed or lost, and then pass it on to others

> **2 TIMOTHY 1:13** Hold on to the pattern of wholesome teaching you learned from me—a pattern shaped by the faith and love that you have in Christ Jesus.

Timothy had spent time with Paul, both on his own and with other people. During those times he would have been watching Paul's life and the way he worked. No doubt they discussed many things together, and Timothy heard Paul teaching others. The treasure, the truth, the faith, had been passed on to him. Paul tells him to "retain" or keep the treasure. He was to make it his own - live it and practice it. Make it part of his life.

> **2 TIMOTHY 1:14** Through the power of the Holy Spirit who lives within us, carefully guard the precious truth that has been entrusted to you.

And then Paul says that Timothy is to guard the treasure that has been entrusted into his care. Paul is about to die. His ministry is over. Now Timothy must take the truth which has been entrusted to him and see that it is not harmed or changed or lost in any way. And Paul says that the Holy Spirit will be helping Timothy with this.

> **2 TIMOTHY 2:2** You have heard me teach things that have been confirmed by many reliable witnesses. Now teach these truths to other trustworthy people who will be able to pass them on to others.

So Timothy is to keep and guard the treasure. But not so he can enjoy the truth for himself. This is a treasure which must be passed on. He is to entrust it to others who can then also keep, guard and pass it on intact.

Paul then uses three illustrations to remind Timothy of some important principles for the task he has been entrusted with. He talks about a soldier, an athlete and a farmer:

- Each of these is a long-term occupation.
- Each one requires careful planning, commitment and consistent effort if the goal is to be reached.
- Each requires discipline and some kind of sacrifice.
- Each brings reward if seen through to the end.

Passing on the Treasure intact takes a long-term, disciplined commitment if the rewards in other people's lives are to be seen.

Just like everything that God sets out to do, in His Word He has provided everything we need to know: for salvation, for the Christian life, the function of a church and for the future. As we consider the task of teaching God's Word to others, we need to be committed to the long-term goal of first keeping, then guarding, and finally entrusting this treasure to others.

? DISCUSSION POINTS

1. The tutorial discusses how God's Word is one body of truth and so needs to be passed on intact. What part would you say learning the culture and language of people has in this picture of passing on truth in its entirety?

2. Today there are many evangelistic methods founded on the principle that 'quicker is always better'. There is an urgency in communicating God's Word, so how can we weigh up how is too long? In your opinion what would be some of the *non-negotiables* - things that could not be left out in the communication of truth?

➡ ACTIVITIES

1. In 2 Timothy 2:3-7 Paul says, *"Endure suffering along with me, as a good soldier of Christ Jesus. ⁴ Soldiers don't get tied up in the affairs of civilian life, for then they cannot please the officer who enlisted them. ⁵ And athletes cannot win the prize unless they follow the rules. ⁶ And hard-working farmers should be the first to enjoy the fruit of their labor. ⁷ Think about what I am saying. The Lord will help you understand all these things."* Reflect on these verses and write your thoughts about what Paul was trying to communicate.

4.5 What is culture?

OBJECTIVES OF THIS TUTORIAL

This tutorial introduces the basic concept of 'culture', and discusses what it is.

Introduction

We are going to begin by defining a few terms and considering some of the key processes and concepts embodied by the word, "culture." Before we look at any culture in particular, it is helpful to understand what culture in general is, and how it works. We are going to focus on the relationship between the invisible aspects of culture; the underlying values and assumptions of a society, and culture that can be seen; the specific behaviors that derive from those values. In other words, how does what people think effect how they act?

It is important to understand that what people do and say in a particular culture is not just arbitrary and spontaneous, but it is consistent with what people in that culture value and believe in. By knowing people's values and beliefs, you can come to expect and predict their behavior.

Once people are no longer catching you off guard with their actions, and once you are no longer simply reacting to their behavior, you are well on your way to successful cultural adjustment. Once you accept that people behave the way they do for a reason - whatever you may think of that reason - you can go beyond simply reacting to that behavior and figure out how to work with it. Knowing where behavior is coming from doesn't mean that you have to like or accept it, but it should mean that you're no longer surprised by it - and that's a big step toward successful interaction.

Cultural assumptions

Imagine that you have been invited to a meal in your neighbor's home. You would probably feel confident that you know how to behave politely in that situation. Your mother probably taught you as a child what was expected of you, and your behavior has been refined since then by many experiences of dining with others. You know to do things like greeting your host politely, asking where you should sit at the dining table, holding your knife and fork correctly...etc. You probably don't even think about those kinds of things any more. But what if your neighbors had recently come to your country from Senegal? There are many points of etiquette that a Senegalese person knows constitute polite behavior that you might not know. These are the things that their parents would have taught them or that have been modeled for them that they don't even think about anymore.

For example, in a Senegalese visiting and dining situation you should begin by greeting the family and taking time to ask about the health and welfare of family members. You should wait to be shown to your seat, and not just sit down wherever you want, because seating is often a matter of hierarchy. The meal might be served on the floor or a low table, so you should sit cross-legged, trying not let your feet touch the food mat. You shouldn't start to eat until the oldest male starts to eat. Food is often served from a communal bowl, and you should eat from the section of the bowl in front of you and you would never reach across the bowl to get something from the other side. And eat only with your right hand. Your hosts will urge you to take second helpings, and you should always sample each dish that is offered. Leave a little food on your plate or in your section of the communal bowl, because this shows that you have had enough to eat and that your hosts have looked after you well. And, people usually stay for at least half an hour after eating, to talk and show that the personal relationship with your hosts is important to you.

So, even though you might very much want to be polite and show respect to your neighbors, there is a real risk of you acting in a way that might seem to them to be very impolite, and possibly even annoying or offensive. If you don't know what is "polite" and "respectful", you can't communicate that to your neighbors, even with the best intentions.

That people from two different cultures can view the same behavior differently is precisely what makes cross-cultural encounters so challenging and problematic.

The iceberg

Culture has been compared to an iceberg. Part of the iceberg is visible - above the waterline - but there is a larger, invisible section below the water line. Culture has some aspects that are observable. These are the things people do and say - their behavior. But there are other aspects of culture that can only be suspected, imagined, or worked out by instinct. So, like an iceberg, the part of culture that we can observe is only a small part of a much bigger whole. The aspects of culture that might be described as being 'below the waterline' are things that have to do with values, beliefs, thoughts and opinions.

TUTORIAL 4.5

Below is a list of some common features of culture. Rewrite the list, dividing it into two sections - things you consider to be above the waterline (observable behavior), and those things that are not observable.

- facial expressions
- religious beliefs
- religious rituals
- the importance of time
- paintings
- values
- literature
- child raising beliefs
- what leadership means
- gestures
- festivals and holidays
- the concept of justice
- what friendship means
- what is modest or immodest
- popular foods
- common eating habits
- education standards
- understanding of the natural world
- the concept of self
- the accepted work ethic
- what is considered beautiful
- music
- types of dress
- general worldview
- view of personal space
- rules of social etiquette

Suggested answers for this exercise are at the end of the tutorial.

You might notice that there is a relationship between observable behavior - things that appear above the waterline - and those things that are not observable. In most cases, the invisible aspects of culture influence or cause the visible ones. For example, religious beliefs often motivate the form of festivals, holidays or rituals. Rules of social etiquette influence common eating habits, and child raising beliefs and the accepted work ethic, influence education.

If your desire is to learn to communicate clearly cross-culturally, it is important to take the necessary time to learn to understand those deeper, hidden things that are below the surface of observable behavior.

Linking values to behavior

We saw how some aspects of culture show up in people's behavior, and that many other aspects of culture are invisible - such as thoughts, feelings, and beliefs. We saw that these two areas, the visible and the hidden, are actually related to each other, and that the values and beliefs that can't be seen are what influence behavior.

If you want to understand where behavior comes from - to understand why people behave the way they do - then you will have to learn about values and beliefs. The behavior of people from another culture may seem strange to you, but it probably makes sense to them, and vice versa. Our behavior makes sense to us because it is consistent with what we believe or what we think is worthwhile. When we say that what someone has done "makes no sense," what we mean is that their action contradicts what we believe that person really feels or wants.

Behavior	Value or Belief
At a meeting, agreeing with a suggestion you actually think is wrong.	Saving face
Not helping the person next to you on an exam.	Self-reliance
Taking a day off school to attend the wedding of a cousin.	Centrality of family
Keeping on an older member of staff whose performance is weak.	Respect for age
Asking a question to bring out your opinion rather than disagreeing openly.	Indirectness
Asking the boss for his opinion about something that you're an expert in.	Deference to authority
Inviting the cleaning staff to eat lunch with everyone else in your office.	Egalitarianism

Asking people to call you by your first name.	Informality
Disagreeing openly with someone at a meeting.	Directness
Accepting, without question, that something can't be changed.	External Control

Universal, cultural or personal?

All of us have preferences, thoughts about things and certain ways of doing things. Some of these are universal to all people, some are dictated by our culture, and some are just our own personal preferences. So we can say that culture is only one dimension of human behavior. To understand what culture is, it is important to see it in relation to the other two dimensions - the universal and the personal. Let's define them and look at some examples:

Universal refers to ways in which all people in all groups are the same. Some examples:

- Being careful when crossing the road.
- Sleeping regularly.
- Regretting being the cause of an injury to another person.
- Feeling sad at the death of a mother or father.
- Getting food and preparing it.

Cultural refers to what a particular group of people have in common with each other and how they are different from every other group.

Some examples:

- Considering snakes to be sacred.
- Waiting in a queue.
- Respecting older people.
- Eating with chopsticks.
- Being welcoming to strangers.
- Pointing with the bottom lip.
- Smearing ashes on your face in respect of a death.

Personal describes the ways in which each one of us is different from everyone else, including those in our group.

Some examples:

- Sleeping with the window open.

- Liking spicy food.
- Preferring playing soccer to reading a book.
- Not liking large social gatherings.

There are two important things for you to remember:

1. Because of universal behavior, not everything about people in a new culture is going to be different: some of what you already know about human behavior is going to apply in another culture.
2. Because of personal behavior, not everything you learn about another culture is going to apply in equal measure, or at all, to every individual in that culture.

For example, I lived with my family for many years in a small, isolated village in Papua New Guinea. We lived among the people and learned their language and culture. One of the differences in culture we recognized almost immediately was in the area of "privacy". As westerners, we highly valued privacy in our family and personal life - even considering that we had a 'personal life' was evidence of our view of privacy. Although we enjoyed spending a lot of time with the local people, we liked to choose when that time would be. We also liked (or needed) some time when we were just on our own.

Most of our friends in the village did not consider personal privacy in many areas of life to be something to be valued or sought after. Many had not even thought much about it before. However, one local family saw how we lived, and noticed that we valued times when we were alone as a family. They expressed empathy for our feelings about privacy and said that they also liked to have some time alone as a family, and that always being with other people was stressful to them. They said that they liked to keep the inside of their home a 'private place' and that they didn't enjoy people just walking in unannounced. This was a surprise to us, because we assumed that everyone in the village thought about privacy in the same way. In time, as we became closer to people and got to know them on a deeper level, we identified many areas of 'culture' - common behaviors and beliefs that most people in the group shared. But we also noticed many cases of personal preference as well. Even in that isolated, very homogenous cultural situation, there were other cases of people who did not always follow the cultural norms.

? DISCUSSION POINTS

1. Most people do not naturally look at their own culture objectively, but rather act within their culture without considering why they do things. Why do you think that is?

2. What would you say are some of the most formative influences on your own country's cultural values - where did they come from?

ACTIVITIES

1. The differences between universal, cultural, and personal behaviors occur in all cultures. Try to find examples of each in your local situation. Spend some time in a public community place observing people, and note four examples of each category of behavior that you observed. For personal behaviors, you may find it easier observing people you know well, such as people at your work, church or among your family and friends.

ANSWERS

The Iceberg

These are aspect of culture that are visible - above the waterline:

> facial expressions, religious rituals, paintings, literature, gestures, festivals and holidays, popular foods, common eating habits, education standards, music, types of dress, rules of social etiquette.

These items are in the invisible part:

> religious beliefs, the importance of time, values, child raising beliefs, what leadership means, the concept of justice, what friendship means, what is modest or immodest, understanding of the natural world, the concept of self, the accepted work ethic, what is considered beautiful, general worldview, view of personal space.

4.6 Understanding culture

OBJECTIVES OF THIS TUTORIAL

This tutorial continues with the theme of 'culture' by examining how we learn cultural behaviors and how we interpret things differently depending on our culture.

Enculturation

How do we learn all the different behaviors that are regarded as right and wrong in our society? This process, known as 'enculturation' or 'cultural conditioning', is something that is universal to all cultures. In every culture people must learn to function together effectively in order to survive, and to seek to live a comfortable, profitable existence together. People develop rules for functioning together, some of these rules are universal and others vary from culture to culture. These rules of behavior are passed on from generation to generation, so that people learn or acquire them throughout their lives. There are many specific behaviors that people learn or acquire, and they vary greatly from group to group.

We noted in the last tutorial that behavior is always linked to an underlying value or belief. So when people are learning cultural behaviors, they are also learning and internalizing the values and beliefs behind those behaviors. When you understand how this process works, you can then understand how two people from different cultures can behave in radically different ways and both be completely convinced they are right. This can be one of the most helpful things to learn if you intend to live and work effectively in another culture.

How do people acquire their culture?

Enculturation happens mostly during early childhood. But adults also continue to be culturally conditioned as they learn new behaviors, or refine existing behaviors, throughout their life.

There are differences between adult and childhood cultural conditioning. During childhood, infants and young children learn the basic activities of life such as eating, walking, talking, dressing, bathing, etc. But during adulthood, people learn new, more complex behaviors or new ways to perform already conditioned behaviors. For example, an adult might learn to eat with chopsticks rather than with a knife and fork, or they might learn to be less direct in the way they communicate in certain situations.

Though the steps are the same in each case, one difference in adult enculturation - especially when an adult moves from one culture to a new one - is that it often requires *un*learning or *un*acquiring behavior that was already acquired during childhood conditioning. This process for adults can take longer and be more difficult.

Here are five steps that have been identified in the process of cultural conditioning:

1. *Observation/Instruction:* At this stage, you are only beginning to become aware of a particular behavior but have not yet tried to do it yourself. For example - eating with chopsticks: you may have watched people doing it, or someone may have told you how to do it.

2. *Imitation:* Now you actually try to carry out the activity: you sit down at a table and begin eating with chopsticks (or trying to). At this stage, it is awkward for you, and you're trying not to make mistakes. You may have difficulty concentrating on anything else, because all your attention is focused on eating.

3. *Reinforcement:* As you eat, people encourage you when you do it right and correct you when you are wrong. You have a chance to put into practice what they tell you and you try to improve. You will also be picking up some of the associated values with this behavior - such as how important it is for people to see that you to learn to eat 'properly'.

4. *Internalization:* Without needing much reinforcement, over time and with practice, you now know how to eat with chopsticks. You will still have to pay attention to what you're doing, but not as much as during stages 2 and 3. You begin to feel like you fit in better in social situations that involve eating, and the attention isn't so much on you learning this skill.

5. *Spontaneous Manifestation:* Now you're able to eat 'in the right way' without paying any conscious attention to what you're doing. It comes naturally: as you eat, you're aware of other things, not the act of eating. You have expressed some of your personal values to your local friends; that it is important for you to become a real part of you new community, that you want to learn, that you enjoy and respect their culture.

It's all in the way that you see it

We all observe reality - see things as they are - but then our minds interpret what our eyes see, and give it meaning. The mind of a person from one culture is going to be different in many ways from the mind of a person from another culture, so their interpretation of what they are seeing - the meaning that they derive from the same reality - is going to be different. This is one of the most fundamental of all cross-cultural problems: the fact that two people look upon the same reality, the same example of behavior, and 'see' two entirely different things. So any behavior in a cross-cultural situation should be interpreted in two ways:

- the meaning given to it by the person who does the action, and
- the meaning given to it by the person who observes the action

When these two meanings are the same, then we can say that the cross-cultural communication has been successful - because the meaning that was intended by the doer, is the one that was understood by the observer. This of course also applies for spoken communication cross-culturally, but we will talk about that more later. For now, we will just think about behaviors.

Different interpretations

To help you to think about the real-life implications of what we have been discussing, on the following page are a few examples of cultural differences in the interpretation of the same behaviors. You have probably come into contact with people of other cultures and may have experienced some cultural misunderstandings yourself. These examples are all from real situations that my family and I have experienced in a variety of cultures around the world.

Read the description of the behavior, and then think about how you would have interpreted it in terms of your own cultural values, beliefs, or perception. Then read what our interpretation was at the time. Finally read the description of the intended meaning of the person who did the behavior. The point here is that until you take time to learn to understand a culture so that you can correctly interpret the intended meaning, misunderstandings are inevitable. Learning culture to that level takes time and effort.

Behavior	Our interpretation	Intended meaning
Two young women at an airport information desk looked away and didn't smile or answer my polite enquiry for directions.	For some reason they have decided to be rude. Maybe there's something about me they don't like? What did I do wrong?	They didn't speak any English so they were trying to manage an awkward situation. They wanted to 'save face' for everyone involved.
A puppy ran up to us trying to be friendly as we were sitting in a village. The people we were visiting yelled and threw stones at it until it ran away.	How could they be so cruel?! We would never treat dogs that way!	The local dogs have rabies and other diseases, so our hosts were protecting us.
We were having a friendly conversation with a guesthouse manager at his front desk when an older man walked in and stood in front of us, taking the manager's attention and interrupting our conversation.	The older man must be a very rude person - maybe for some reason he doesn't like Westerners.	The older gentleman was a local government official who had supported the guest house owners over the years and so was entitled to a 'special relationship'. As an older man, and an official, he was entitled to great respect. We were just ordinary guests.
My husband accidentally bumped his arm on the fur hat of an older man on a crowded bus. Local friends immediately told him to apologize profusely and humbly to the older man.	It seemed like an over reaction - it's only a hat after all, and it was just a very slight bump. There must be something we don't understand here.	It is extremely offensive to show disrespect by touching the head of another person - especially an older man. Local people would be very careful not to let this happen.
We had traveled all day by motorcycle to visit a village and we were hungry. When we arrived we spent over an hour 'chatting' with our hosts before being offered any food.	This seemed inconsiderate to us because they knew we had traveled all day.	The interpersonal relationship was the priority and they were showing that was the most important thing to them. To serve food immediately would have been disrespectful to us.

A meeting was arranged for a certain time, but two local men were over an hour late. When they arrived they said they had been visiting someone else first.	We felt 'let down' and that they had been disrespectful of our meeting. We wondered if they felt negatively about our relationship in some way and were trying to show us that.	They do not have the same view of time as us. The personal relationship with the other people had to be preserved and everyone understands that sometimes you are just late - it isn't a big deal and doesn't mean anything.
A local family were hiking with us on a trail. The woman was carrying a very heavy load on her head and had a baby strapped to her back, while also taking care of another younger child. Her husband was walking in front of her and was only carrying a knife.	How about helping your wife!? You should be ashamed of letting her do all the hard work!	The woman is proud of her strength and ability to work hard. She is demonstrating that she is a 'good wife'. Her husband is proud of her and wouldn't interfere with her carrying out her role.

UNDERSTANDING CULTURE

❓ DISCUSSION POINTS

1. This tutorial discusses how people from different cultures see things from a different point of view. Can you identify some cultural groups within the wider society in which you live - in other words, sub-groups within your country's culture - who might interpret things quite differently from you?

2. Think about some of the subgroups you identified in the question above that exist within your country's culture. How do you think their particular culture was acquired - and why do you think individuals in that particular group have acquired different cultural characteristics from those around them?

➡ ACTIVITIES

1. Try to take note of any instances that you observe this week of misinterpretation of behavior. What were the underlying reasons for the communication breakdown?

2. Read the definitions of culture given in the following short quotations (next page). Then note - in around eight phrases - any idea, concept, or key word that is repeated more than once. Assemble these recurring phrases to give you a good working definition of culture. Because, while the concept of 'culture' has many definitions, most observers agree on certain fundamental characteristics.

Definitions of culture

Culture is the collective programming of the mind which distinguishes the members of one group from another.

- Geert Hofstede

Culture is the shared set of assumptions, values, and beliefs of a group of people by which they organize their common life.

- Gary Wederspahn

Culture consists in patterned ways of thinking, feeling and reacting. The essential core of culture consists of traditional ideas and especially their attached values.

- Clyde Kluckhohn

Culture consists of concepts, values, and assumptions about life that guide behavior and are widely shared by people...[These] are transmitted generation to generation, rarely with explicit instructions, by parents...and other respected elders.

- Richard Brislin & Tomoko Yoshida

Culture is the outward expression of a unifying and consistent vision brought by a particular community to its confrontation with such core issues as the origins of the cosmos, the harsh unpredictability of the natural environment, the nature of society, and humankind's place in the order of things.

- Edward Hall

Culture is an integrated system of learned behavior patterns that are characteristic of the members of any given society. Culture refers to the total way of life for a particular group of people. It includes [what] a group of people thinks, says, does and makes—its customs, language, material artifacts and shared systems of attitudes and feelings.

- Robert Kohls

4.7 The Concept of Self

> **OBJECTIVES OF THIS TUTORIAL**
>
> This tutorial focuses on one of the foundational concepts of any culture, the concept of self. The way people think about 'who they are' varies greatly between cultures. So we will take a look at the two 'poles' of this concept, individualism and collectivism.

Introduction

Culture is a complex concept, with many dimensions and facets, but one of the most important building blocks of any culture is the 'concept of the self'. One of the most significant ways in which cultures differ is in how they view this concept. Later we will look at some other foundational cultural concepts - societal obligations, the concept of time, and who is in control. These are all significant concepts in shaping many cultural differences.

Not everything that people do can be explained by these fundamental concepts, but they are often the source of the beliefs or values that are behind a wide range of thought and behavior. If you come to understand the way people of another culture view these fundamental areas, it will help you to understand why people think and behave the way they do. And if you discover more about how these concepts are viewed in your own cultural community, it might give you more insight into why you think and behave the way you do.

The concept of self is how a person feels that they fit into their society or community. At one end of the scale, a person thinks of themselves as an individual - everyone is expected to look after him/herself and his/her immediate family. This is called an individualistic view, and cultures that are generally this way are called individualistic cultures. At the other end of the scale, a person views themselves as an integral part of a group - family, community, society - and so they have multiple obligations and close connections with others. This is called a collectivist view, and cultures that are generally this way are called collectivist cultures.

We will describe both of these views and give some examples of each to illustrate them.

The concept of self in practice

It is a common experience for people living in a cross-cultural situation to come up against things that they feel are "just not fair" or "just not right". Sometimes that is true - there are going to be things that are wrong in every culture - but sometimes our reactions can stem from not understanding the fundamental values of another culture. Once we come to understand them, we may even agree with those underlying values, such as 'the importance of family', for example. But because these values motivate different behaviors in another culture, we probably won't easily recognize them for what they are. In fact it can be almost impossible for us to see some things from the other person's point of view unless we dig deeper and try to understand the underlying values involved.

The concept of self is one of these deep concepts that motivate behavior - so we have to try to understand how another culture differs from our own in this area if we want to understand people's behavior. We will take a look at an example to try to illustrate how the concept of self can play out in a real situation.

Imagine that your local community group has decided to make a community garden area. For six weeks, you and the three other people working with you have been working on fencing, a garden shed, and some large garden beds. On your team, Mia had the most free time, so she did 40% of the work. You and Kieran each did 25% of the work and Ethan did 10% of the work. Now the work is finished. A local business that had donated materials has also benefited from advertising using the garden project. So this business has decided to give the four of you a cash payment of $20,000 for your work. How do you think this money should be distributed?

How did you make your decision - what was it based on?

Because of my cultural background, which is *individualistic*, I would divide the money according to how much each person worked. So if I was dividing the money, Mia would get $8000, you and Kieran would each get $5000, and Ethan would get $2000. This would definitely seem to me to be the 'right' and the 'fair' thing to do.

In a *collectivist* culture, the money in this situation would often be divided equally - each person on the team would get $5000.

People in collectivist cultures will prioritize the good of the group over any individual's good, even if it is their own. This is because they believe that the best way to guarantee personal survival or security is to make sure that the group thrives and prospers. If the individual prospers and the group does not, then ultimately that does not work out well for the individual anyway.

If I came from a collectivist cultural background, it would be more important and comforting to me if everyone in my group could benefit as much as possible from the cash offered for the garden work. So each person would get $5000. No matter how much or how little each person was able to work, the whole group would benefit equally from the exercise of building the garden. If Ethan, who was only able to do 10% of the work, only got $2000, I would worry about his financial well-being. And if he suffered from financial need, then he might not be able to help in the future and we would all suffer.

Individualism and collectivism

The example of the community garden illustrates how different concepts of self can influence real life situations. Now we will look at more theoretical descriptions of the two poles of the concept of self - individualism and collectivism. Remember that no culture is exclusively individualist or collective - and there are distinct individuals within each type of culture. But most cultures and people tend to be more one than the other.

Individualist

The individual identifies primarily with self. They would seek to satisfy their own needs before those of the group. The well-being of the group is only guaranteed by each individual looking after and taking care of themselves and being self-sufficient. Independence and self-reliance are greatly stressed and valued. People only have loose connections with others. In general, people tend to distance themselves psychologically and emotionally from each other. A person might choose to join groups, but group membership is not essential to a person's identity or success. Individualist characteristics are often more closely associated with men and with people in urban settings.

Collectivist

The individual identifies primarily as a part of a group. A person's identity is in their membership and role in a group, such as their family or work team. The survival and success of the group guarantees the well-being of the individual. You protect yourself by considering the needs and feelings of others. Harmony and the interdependence of group members are stressed and valued. Group members are relatively close psychologically and emotionally, but distant toward non-group members. Collectivist characteristics are often associated with women and people in rural settings.

Influences on everyday life

The way that people view their identity has a broad impact on the way people of that culture function on a day to day level. Below are some examples of behaviors from an individualistic, and then from a collectivist culture.

These behaviors would point toward a culture being more individualistic:

- People give parties for a wide circle of friends. A party means, generally, superficial contact with a lot of people. Collectivists would tend to associate more intensely with a few people.

THE CONCEPT OF SELF

- Many kinds of individual awards are given, e.g, school awards and sporting awards, etc. This kind of award singles out an individual above everyone else.
- People are promoted based on production, results, sales figures. Rewards are based on what you do, rather than on who you are (which is more collectivist).
- Contracts are used in business. Because in an individualist culture people are after personal rather than group benefit, contracts keep people honest. In a collectivist culture people will be honest based on mutual accountability (if they are not honest, the group will punish them).
- People feel a need for autonomy. Individuals need their independence and react negatively to being controlled too much by others.
- People change jobs frequently. Their loyalty is to themselves rather than to an organization.
- People believe that directness and even conflict is often a good thing because it 'clears the air'. Collectivists avoid conflict because it could damage group harmony.
- Short-term relationships are common. Long-term relationships tie the individual down; also individualists move a lot, are less loyal to a place or other people.
- It's okay to stand out or to be different to other people. Collectivists prefer self-effacement and harmony with others.
- It's common for parents to ask their children what they want to wear or what they want to eat or what they want to do. Fostering independence and taking responsibility for self is encouraged from a young age.
- Self-help books are popular (instead of "helping others" books). The individual is responsible to look after themselves.
- People would often ask 'what can I bring' to a dinner invitation. In a collectivist culture, the host would provide for everyone, and then expect to be provided for in turn later on.

These behaviors in a culture would point toward it being more collectivist:

- People answer the phone by giving the name of the organization. Giving *your* name would be more individualist.
- Intergroup rivalry and competition is strong. Within a group, collectivists stick together; so therefore they can be very competitive with other groups.
- People adhere to tradition. Because the older, more senior people are listened to, the more traditional ideas are often promoted.

- There is a need for affiliation. People are defined by what they belong to, and who their group is, not by individual characteristics or achievements.

- Face saving is important. Saving face - not embarrassing or humiliating someone - maintains harmony, which is the glue that keeps the group together

- Decisions are made by consensus. There must be agreement so no one feels left out (as opposed to 'majority rules', which leaves the minority out).

- The language has very specific words for relationships between people, for example, one word for mother's brother, another for father's brother. The need to be more specific about relationships is more important to collectivists.

- Marriages are arranged or agreed upon by family members rather than just the man and woman involved. These arrangements keep the group, and family, happy (which in turn keeps the individual happy).

Individualist and collectivist cultures

It isn't a good idea to generalize about the culture of specific countries, because there may be many different cultures represented in any one country - as is the case in Australia. However, in the diagram below, countries are placed on the scale of individualism and collectivism according to their general culture. The more individualistic cultures are higher on the diagram.

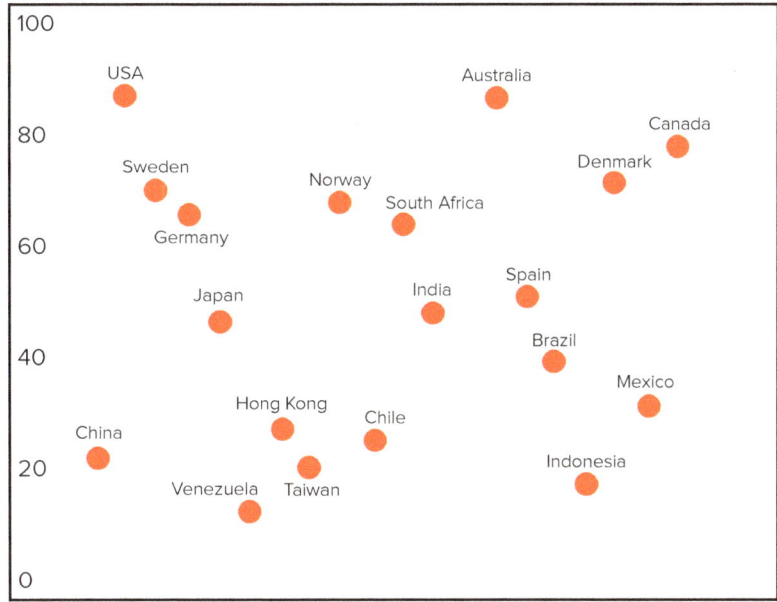

THE CONCEPT OF SELF

 **DISCUSSION POINTS**

1. Have you thought much before about the way you view the concept of self and where that concept comes from?

2. What are some of the major factors that you think might have contributed to your personal concept of identity - of who you are and how you fit in with the community around you?

3. Do you think that the effect that God's Word has on someone's identity - on their concept of self - can be considered a 'cultural' influence or is it something apart from culture?

ACTIVITIES

1. Look at each of the following statements and decide first if you agree with the statement, then if it would be more likely to be said by someone from an individualist culture or a collectivist culture:

- Being straight with people is always best in the end.
- It takes a long time to make a new friend.
- If my brother or sister did wrong, I would defend them to other people.
- Confrontation almost always causes more problems than it solves.
- Managers should be hired on the basis of the skills they have and previous experience in similar jobs.
- I am embarrassed by individual recognition.
- In the end, you can always rely on other people.
- I expect people to judge me by my achievements.
- If I took a job with a new company, I would be afraid that my employer might lose face.

4.8 Discovering your own culture

OBJECTIVES OF THIS TUTORIAL

This tutorial attempts to help you to look at the culture that you have grown up with in a more objective way, particularly focusing on the underlying values of your culture.

Introduction

In this tutorial, we have used Australian culture as the example. If you have another cultural background, you can use the categories explored here to research your own cultural values. Just use the headings and try to research similar information about your own culture. Also, you could think about how your culture differs from Australian culture.

Any culture is made up of individual people, each one unique in their own way. So no Australian is exactly like any other Australian, but a handful of core values and beliefs do underlie and permeate the national culture of Australia. These values and beliefs don't apply across the board in every situation - and individuals may even act in ways that directly contradict or flaunt commonly shared values and beliefs - but they are still at the heart of the Australian cultural ethos. In this tutorial we will try to discover some of these values and beliefs, and the characteristic behaviors that come from them.

Our view of ourselves 1

Following is a short guide to Australian culture provided by a university. It is designed to help international students to "fit in" as they study in Australia. As you read it, think about the cultural values that are implied and how a new student contemplating living and studying in Australia might feel as they read it.

Australian Culture

from the University of Newcastle International Students page, 2014

There is no such thing as a 'typical Australian,' and during your time here you will come across a wide range of social customs, habits and perspectives of life that may be very different from your own culture. Here are a few tips to help you adjust:

Addressing People

As a student it is socially accepted to greet fellow students or people the same age or younger than you by their first names. It is common in Australia for people to have nicknames, which are used amongst friends. If you are addressing people senior to you, call them by their surname with their title of Mr, Mrs or Ms, until you know them well enough to call them by their first name.

Greetings

Australia is generally a relaxed, informal society, so you might hear fellow students and friends greet each other with: 'Hello', 'Hi' or 'Hey, how's it going?' If you find yourself in a more formal environment it is customary to shake the hand of those you meet, and greet them with the formal greeting of 'good morning', 'good afternoon' or 'good evening'. However, if this is culturally unacceptable for you, let the person you are meeting know and they will generally be happy to accommodate your need. Use this as an opportunity to share your culture with the local community.

Goodbye

In an informal setting it is ok to simply say: 'See you later,' or 'See you around.' In a more formal setting or the first time you meet someone you might like to say: 'It was a pleasure to meet you,' or 'It was nice to meet you.'

Please and Thank you

When you would like something, it is customary to say 'please'. Once you receive something or when something is provided, say 'thank you'. Australians are very big users of please and thank you.

Slang

Australians insert slang into daily conversation, and it is done almost unconsciously. Don't panic! Here are a few examples:

- *G'day:* Good day/Hello
- *See ya later:* See you later/Goodbye
- *You right?:* Do you need assistance?
- *D'you reckon?:* Do you think so?
- *Good on ya!:* Well done!
- *It's my shout!:* It is my turn to buy you a meal or a drink. If someone 'shouts' you something it is customary to return the gesture.
- *Tute:* Tutorial

Eye Contact

It is customary to engage in direct eye contact with those who are talking to you, and when you are talking to them. This is not disrespectful, but a sign of interest and sincerity. Australians will make direct eye contact with everyone they come into contact with.

Personal Space

Australians like their personal space. This doesn't mean that Australians are unapproachable, but we do like our freedom. When talking to someone, be mindful of your position. Generally an arm's length is a good distance to converse with someone, any closer and both you and the person may feel uncomfortable.

Humor

Australians are known for a 'dry' or 'laconic' sense of humor, involving light hearted banter which is commonly referred to as 'stirring'. Don't panic if you don't understand Australian humor straight away; as your knowledge about the country grows, you too will be joining in on the laughs!

Social Invitations

If you receive a verbal or written invitation to an event, it is customary to RSVP to the host to inform them of your acceptance or decline of the invite. If you are asked to 'join' or 'go with' a group to a social outing you are expected to pay for your own expenses.

If you are invited to a friend's house for a meal, it is customary to ask if you could contribute to the meal. This just might be something simple, like a bottle of drink or a platter of food. Some parties maybe BYO, which means bring your own food or drink. Invitations may include 'bring a plate,' meaning bring a plate of food to share with other guests.

Dress

Dress in Australia tends to be casual with jeans and t-shirts. Some work places require business attire, while occasions marked as 'formal,' will include the type of dress required.

Queuing

If you are waiting for a taxi, a bus, a ticket, service, or a cashier, it is customary to wait your turn and not to push. Pushing and not waiting for your turn will not be tolerated.

Punctuality

While Australian society is relaxed, it is customary to keep your appointments and turn up on time. If you are running late for an appointment or occasion, always call to explain before the event.

Equality

Australians believe that everyone is equal, regardless of age, gender, ethnicity or social standing. Australians enjoy equal social, legal and political rights, which are protected by the Australian Constitution.

Our view of ourselves 2

Below is the agreement called "Australian Values Statement" which applicants for an Australian visa (long term visas) are required to sign before being granted a visa (from the Australian Government Department of Immigration and Citizenship). Notice as you read it the importance that is placed on societal values in people wanting to become Australian citizens.

Australian Values Statement

You must sign this statement if you are aged 18 years or over.

I confirm that I have read, or had explained to me, information provided by the Australian Government on Australian society and values.

I understand:

- Australian society values respect for the freedom and dignity of the individual, freedom of religion, commitment to the rule of law, Parliamentary democracy, equality of men and women and a spirit of egalitarianism that embraces mutual respect, tolerance, fair play and compassion for those in need and pursuit of the public good
- Australian society values equality of opportunity for individuals, regardless of their race, religion or ethnic background
- the English language, as the national language, is an important unifying element of Australian society.

I undertake to respect these values of Australian society during my stay in Australia and to obey the laws of Australia.

I understand that, if I should seek to become an Australian citizen:

- Australian citizenship is a shared identity, a common bond which unites all Australians while respecting their diversity
- Australian citizenship involves reciprocal rights and responsibilities. The responsibilities of Australian Citizenship include obeying Australian laws, including those relating to voting at elections and serving on a jury.

If I meet the legal qualifications for becoming an Australian citizen and my application is approved I understand that I would have to pledge my loyalty to Australia and its people.

Culture in casual expressions

Some insight into cultural values can be gained by examining common expressions people use in everyday conversation. These common expressions often reflect widely shared values or beliefs. Below are some common Australian sayings, with a description of the value or belief that they might be expressing.

- "He thinks he's better than so and so"
- "She's always putting on airs"
- "That person should be cut down to size"
- "He's got tickets on himself"

Value/belief: Egalitarianism. Australians are sensitive and resistant to class distinctions - 'Cut the tall poppy' - there are consequently relatively few class differences. This can sometimes manifest itself in Australians seeming to others to be disrespectful, to resent superiors and to resist control, or to prefer to bargain with management because they assume subordinates share equal interests and capabilities.

- "You're not wrong"
- "I don't think much of that"
- "That's not bad" (meaning 'that's good')
- "It's pretty ordinary" (meaning 'it's quite bad')

Value/belief: These kinds of expressions using understatement are often used to indicate familiarity and a closer relationship. Some other common examples are diminutives - *arvo* (afternoon), *barbie* (barbecue), *smoko* (cigarette break), *Aussie* (Australian) and *pressie* (present/gift). This may also be done with people's names to create nicknames, e.g, *Lozza* (for Laurie or Lauren), or "Clarky" for Mr. Clark. Sometimes to others, Australians can seem terse, non-committal and understated or overly casual in conversation.

- "No worries!"
- "G'day mate"
- "Good on you"

Value/belief: Casual optimism, amiability, friendliness and an expectation of shared attitudes (a proneness to easy 'mateship').

- "Fair go"
- "C,mon give us a break"

Value/belief: A reasonable chance, a fair deal. Everyone is entitled to consideration and to getting a fair deal, all citizens have a right to fair treatment.

- "My mates are coming over"
- "You can rely on your mates"

Value/belief: "Mateship". Value inherent qualities in others (rather than external achievements). Friends and membership groups take a long time to establish. Relationships are long-lasting and meaningful. Friendship involves a very strong sense of obligation - you always help your mates no matter what - expression of comradeship and equality.

- "Stand on your own two feet"
- "He's doing it tough"

Value/belief: Respect for "battlers" - making ends meet and getting through tough times without whingeing. People who don't pull their weight are "bludgers".

- "You've got to laugh" (or you'd cry...)
- "Don't worry - she'll be right"
- "Such is life"

Value/belief: 'Whatever is wrong will right itself with time' - a philosophical acceptance of the bad things that happen in life. This could be considered to be either an optimistic or apathetic outlook.

Can you think of other common expressions, ones you use yourself or that are common in your family? Write them down and then consider the value or belief they represent.

Cultural characteristics

Below is a list of values or cultural characteristics that have been said to be common to Australians. As you read the list think about yourself - do you think all or some of these apply to you? Also, think about whether in your own case, you would tend to put these characteristics down to individual "personality" rather than a shared "culture".

- They enjoy disagreement, and don't care what others think.
- They use humor frequently, often injecting a certain amount of cynicism or irony to any situation, and are inclined to use humor under stress.
- They are generally 'laid back'.
- Work rarely comes between friends.
- Overtime isn't accepted unless the reason is extremely important.
- They need to be convinced of the usefulness before the value of the work is seen.
- Evaluate their own behavior based on their own feelings and preferences (rather than outside influences).
- Tend to be inflexible.
- Achievement is not so important; position and honors are minimized.
- More free time very important; salary less so.
- Are willing to take risks - to 'have a go' at a thing.
- Only begrudgingly give credit and don't expect praise.
- Comfortable with conflict and invite argument.

Sources of Australian Values

We have identified some of the values that are common to many Australians. In any culture, it is important to realize that values don't "just happen" - they are formed in response to real factors in the history, geography or development of a country - our values and beliefs are a result of our national experience. This is true of every county's culture. So where do Australian values come from?

The beginning of an Australian national identity dates back to the time of early European settlement. Influences on the developing culture at that time comprised a composite of British or Anglo-Saxon heritage, and the harsh conditions of settlement. So, physical toughness, mateship, and the ability to withstand hardship were foundational in the development of an Australian identity. Over time, other factors of historical significance have influenced the development of a national identity - for instance, factors related to the gold rush days; Federation; the Depression; the World Wars and the development of an ANZAC tradition; immigration; and the internationalist era of today. Trends that emerged in the 1970s and 1980s that provided an impetus for change in national identity included multiculturalism, Aboriginal nationalism, and republicanism.

Today, it is very evident that Australia's multiculturalism has influenced all aspects of Australian life, including business, the arts, cooking, sense of humor and sporting tastes. The immigration program - for skilled and family migrants and a humanitarian program for refugees and asylum seekers - has received more than 6.5 million migrants from every continent. The population tripled in six decades to around 21 million in 2010, including people originating from 200 countries. Today, more than 43% of Australians were either born overseas or have one parent who was born overseas. The population is also highly urbanized, with more than 75% of Australians living in urban centers, largely along the coast.

DISCOVERING YOUR OWN CULTURE

? DISCUSSION POINTS

1. How do you feel about increasing multiculturalism and the fact that your country might be losing a cohesive "national cultural identity" with the increase in immigration?

2. Some of the values presented in this tutorial could be called more "traditional" Australian values. Have you seen those values in your own country? If so, have they been changing the last ten years, and how have they changed?

3. The statement has been made, that *"Australians tend to resent any authority that takes a form in which they can have no input. If they sense that decisions are being made with no chance for them to have a say, they will react negatively, even illogically against those decisions"*. Do you see this cultural characteristic evident in the context of the local church and if so, how is it dealt with?

➡ ACTIVITIES

1. Imagine that you are at the airport and you start talking with a couple newly arrived from overseas who tell you they are planning to stay for two years for work. They ask you "tell us about your country." You've got time to make three points about your culture. What three things would you tell them?

2. Find someone who was born in another country and has settled in your home country. Have a conversation with them about cultural differences. Try to find out from them if there are any specific behaviors, beliefs or values:

- that have been difficult for them to understand or accept in your culture.
- that they have retained from their home culture and may be unwilling to change.
- that they hold, but that might be difficult for people in your country to accept.

4.9 Personal vs. societal obligations

OBJECTIVES OF THIS TUTORIAL

This tutorial explores another fundamental area of culture: personal versus societal obligations, or the conflict between individual and social ethics. It defines the two poles of this dimension, *universalism* and *particularism*.

An accident

You are in a car driven by a close friend when he hits a pedestrian. There are no other witnesses and the pedestrian is bruised but not badly hurt. The speed limit is 40km an hour, but you saw that your friend was driving at 55. His lawyer tells you that if you will testify under oath that your friend was driving under 40, he will suffer no serious consequences.

Would you testify that your friend was driving under 40kms an hour? Yes, or no? What do you think *most* people in your culture would do?

The percentage of Americans who said they would not falsely testify to help their friend is 96%. The percentage of Venezuelans who said they would not is 34%. Why do you think there is such a great difference between the Venezuelan and American percentages?

There could be many explanations for the gap here, but one of them almost certainly is a cultural difference between being a universalist (many Americans) and a particularist (many Venezuelans). Universalists tend to feel that right is right, regardless of circumstances, while particularists tend to feel you always have to take circumstances into account. The person in trouble here is your friend, so that would have a bearing on how you would behave in that situation.

The responsibilities of friendship differ from culture to culture. Think about how this exhibits itself in your culture. You will probably find examples of both universalism and particularism, but think about what would be considered the cultural norm - the "right thing" - in the community in which you live. How should a friend be treated in comparison to family members, for example?

Differing views of responsibilities or obligations is obviously an area that can cause misunderstandings or conflict in cross-cultural situations. If you are trying to make friends in a new community, it is helpful to learn to understand the expectations and responsibilities of a friend. In some cultures, friendship requires similar obligations to being a member of the family, whereas in others, friendship has little or no obligation attached.

Universalism and Particularism

People in any culture struggle with how to balance obligations to family, friends, and colleagues on the one hand, and to the wider society on the other. Cultures differ in how they distinguish between obligations to in-group and out-group members. So when personal obligations and societal obligations conflict, different cultures handle the situation in different ways.

No culture is exclusively universalist or particularist, but cultures do tend to be *more* one than the other, and while the attitudes of individuals in a given culture will vary, the focus here as we define the two different attitudes is on the culture as a whole.

Here are brief descriptions of each way of thinking:

Universalism

There are absolutes that apply across the board, regardless of circumstances or the particular situation. Wherever possible, you should try to apply the same rules to everyone in similar situations. To be fair is to treat everyone alike and not make exceptions for family, friends, or members of your in-group. Where possible, you should lay your personal feelings aside and look at the situation objectively. While life isn't necessarily fair, we can make it more fair by treating people the same way. High universalism countries, where there are formal rules and strict adherence to business contracts, are: US, UK, Germany, Sweden, Australia, Switzerland, Canada.

Particularism

How you behave in a given situation depends on the circumstances. You treat family, friends, and your in-group in the best way you can, and you let the rest of the world take care of itself. Your in-group will protect you. There can't be absolutes because everything depends on who you're dealing with in each situation. No one expects life to be fair. Exceptions will always be made for certain people. High particularism countries, where legal contracts can be changed and people deal differently with people based on how well they know them, are: China, Indonesia, Venezuela, South Korea, Russia, India.

Universalism and Particularism in conflict

It is important for you to become aware of the differences in these two poles of thinking if you intend to live in a cross-cultural situation. As you settle in to your new culture and community, there may be times when a conflict or offence arises and you will simply have no idea why. It is a good idea to evaluate what happened and to try to pinpoint the cause.

Many misunderstandings can be traced back to differences in fundamental values, such as the universalist and particularist view we are discussing here. It is almost impossible for a person who has never been exposed to another culture to understand that people think differently on a very deep level, and to see things from the other person's perspective. So, by becoming aware that there are deep differences, you are equipping yourself to understand 'what went wrong' in a cross-cultural situation, and to learn to communicate and behave in an appropriate way in your new community. In any difficult situation it is always good practice to ask a local friend, "How could I have dealt with that better?" and to listen carefully to what they say for the underlying values that are expressed.

Now we are going to look at some statements to help you to identify the universalist and particularist view. In each set of four statements below, one statement is the 'odd one out', and the other three reflect either universalist or particularist views. Pick out the odd statement, and decide which view it represents. The answers follow.

1. Objectivity, not letting personal feelings affect decision making, is possible and desirable.
2. A deal is a deal, whatever happens.
3. Principles have to get bent once in a while.
4. The law is the law.

The third one is particularist; the other three are universalist because, 1: particularists would say personal feelings would have to be taken into account, 2: deals change when circumstances change for particularists, 4: for particularists, the law depends on who you are.

1. You don't compromise on principles.
2. Friends expect preferential treatment.
3. Subjectivity is the rule.
4. The logic of the heart is what counts.

The first one is universalist; the other three are particularist because, 2: this is a key particularist principle, 3: particularists are subjective; universalists are objective, 4: universalist logic is of the head, not the heart.

PERSONAL VS. SOCIETAL OBLIGATIONS

1. People tend to hire friends and associates.
2. Consistency is desirable and possible.
3. Logic of the head is important.
4. Exceptions to the rule should be minimized.

The first one is particularist; the other three are universalist because, 2: particularists avoid consistency because things are relative, 3: particularist logic is of the heart, 4: particularists live by exceptions; there are no absolutes.

1. Friends protect friends.
2. Life is neat, not messy.
3. Written contracts are not necessary.
4. This attitude is more consistent with collectivism.

The second one is universalist; the other three are particularist because, 1: friends can always be trusted (and you don't do business with strangers anyway), 3: particularist logic says the bond is more important than the facts of the case, 4: collectivists have the same in-group/out-group attitudes as particularists do.

1. Situational ethics are the norm.
2. A deal is a deal, until circumstances change.
3. Deals are made on the basis of personal relationships.
4. Justice is blind.

The fourth one is universalist; the other three are particularist because,
1: this is a key particularist concept; no absolutes, 2: particularists always take circumstances into account, 3: relationships, the personal side of things, are more important than cost, etc.

How about you - Universalist or Particularist?
Now you are familiar with the two poles of this concept, you will have a chance to think of your own behavior in the context of this important cultural dimension. Before reading further, take a moment to decide whether you consider yourself more of a universalist or a particularist.

TUTORIAL 4.9

Following are a number of paired statements (a. and b.). Note the one from each pair which best describes the action you would take or the way you feel about the particular topic. Please choose one or the other even if you think both are true. Try to get as honest an answer as you can by answering quickly without too much thinking.

1a. In hiring someone, I want to know about their technical skills and their educational/professional background.

1b. In hiring, I want to know who the person's family and friends are, who will vouch for this person.

2a. In society, we should help those who are the neediest.

2b. In society, we should help the neediest of those who depend on us.

3a. There are certain absolutes which apply across the board.

3b. There are no absolutes in life; you always have to look at the particular situation.

4a. I would not expect my neighbor, the policeman, to jeopardize his job and not give me a speeding ticket.

4b. I would be very hurt if my neighbor, a policeman, gave me a ticket for speeding.

5a. The courts should mediate conflicts.

5b. People should solve their own conflicts; it's embarrassing if it has to go to court.

6a. In general, people can be trusted.

6b. My closest associates can be trusted absolutely; everyone else is automatically suspect.

7a. Performance reviews should not take personal relations into account.

7b. Performance reviews inevitably take personal relations into account.

8a. Exceptions should be very rare; otherwise, you open the floodgates.

8b. You often have to make exceptions for people because of circumstances.

9a. Contracts guarantee that friends stay friends.

9b. Contracts aren't necessary between friends.

10a. Ethics are ethics no matter who you are dealing with.

10b. What is ethical in a given situation depends on who you are dealing with.

Now that you have made your selections, calculate whether you came out more on the universalist or particularist side. The behaviors described in the "a" statements tend to be more characteristic of universalists. The behaviors described in the "b" statements to be more characteristic of particularists. Is your score here consistent with your self-concept?

Having a view of which side of the pole you tend to be, should help you to know that you will definitely see things differently to someone from a culture that tends toward the opposite view. You will need to think carefully and to work at understanding things from their point of view.

? DISCUSSION POINTS

1. You have an idea of both the universalist and particularist approaches to dealing with obligations. Are there features of each approach that you like or agree with? What?

2. Are there features of each approach you don't like or disagree with? What are they and why?

3. Would you describe the Biblical worldview as being more universalist or more particularist?

➡ ACTIVITIES

1. Look again at the statements, characteristics and definitions in the tutorial. Can you find any specific examples or "proof" of universalist or particularist tendencies in your culture?

2. Find a person from a different cultural background and ask them to help you with a cultural exercise - explain the concepts to them - then read the pairs of statements to them to find out whether they are more universalist or particularist.

4.10 Styles of communication 1

OBJECTIVES OF THIS TUTORIAL

This tutorial examines different styles of communication. It will help you to identify the style of communication that is most common in your culture. The focus will be on two of the most important differences in communication style: *direct* and *indirect* communication.

Introduction

Every country has its own way of saying things. The important thing is that which lies behind people's words.

— Freya Stark, The Journey's Echo

Communication - the sending and receiving of messages - is an integral part of culture. Some people go so far as to say that culture is communication. What they probably mean is that since culture is such an important ingredient in all behavior, and so much of behavior is spent in one type of communicating or another, then it's hard to tell where one ends and the other takes over. In any case, whether or not they are one and the same, culture and communication certainly go hand in hand.

In a cross-cultural context, communication, like everything else, is more complicated. It's almost impossible to send a message that does not have at least some cultural content, whether it's in the words themselves, in the way they are said, or in the non-verbal signals that accompany them. And even if it was possible to send a message without any cultural content, it's not possible to receive one without passing it through the filter of your own cultural background. All of which means that people may not interpret everything you say the way you meant it. And vice versa.

Communication problems, especially misunderstanding and misinterpretation, are one of the most common frustrations experienced by people in any cultural setting, particularly where cross-cultural communication is taking place. Different styles of communication mean an increased possibility of misunderstanding.

Styles of communication: indirect and direct

There are quite a few differences in communication style between cultures. The two most important for us to look at are the *indirect (high context)* style, and the *direct (low context)* style.

'Context' refers to the amount of understanding a person can be expected to bring to a particular communication setting. This understanding is often innate and largely unconscious, and cultures vary greatly in how much understanding a person generally brings to a situation.

If a culture is less individualistic, and more collectivist, then everyone knows how people are most likely to behave in a given situation. The shared information level is higher because people know what to expect. This is called a *high context* culture because the shared information level about the context is higher. In high context cultures, people are able to communicate more subtly, or more indirectly. In a low context culture the opposite is true, and so people commonly use more direct communication. Both communication styles are described below:

Indirect (High Context)

In high context cultures, such as Thailand, China, Japan, France and Saudi Arabia, which tend to be homogenous and collectivist, people have a highly developed and refined idea of how most interactions will unfold, of how they and the other person will behave in a particular situation. Because people in high context cultures already know and understand each other quite well, they have a more indirect style of communication. They have less need to be explicit and rely less on words to convey meaning - and especially on the literal meaning of the spoken word - and more on non-verbal communication. People often convey meaning or send messages by manipulating the context rather than using words. Because these cultures tend to be collectivist, people work closely together and know what everyone else knows. Most cultural knowledge is *implicit* (not directly stated) through a myriad of tightly connected, long-term relationships. Information is contained in the context, so it doesn't need to be verbalized directly - conversation often goes around the point. The overriding goal of the communication exchange is maintaining harmony and saving face.

Direct (Low Context)

Direct, or Low Context cultures, such as the US, UK, Canada and Germany are individualistic, logical and task-oriented, tend to be more heterogeneous and accordingly have developed a more direct communication style. Less can be assumed about the other person in a heterogeneous society, and less is known about others in a culture where people prefer independence, self-reliance, and a greater emotional distance from each other and mostly have diverse, discrete, short-term relationships. They can't depend on manipulating context - not doing or not saying something that is always done or said in that situation - or communicating non-verbally to make themselves understood: they must rely more on words, and on those words being interpreted literally. Getting or giving information is the goal of most communication exchanges, so topics are handled straightforwardly.

Relationships are foundational

The structure of how relationships develop and are maintained in different cultures is the foundation for how communication takes place. Relationships in a high-context culture with an indirect communication style will be more group-oriented, because the structure of relationships dictates the communication style. Whereas in a culture where relationships are more individualistic, it will be by nature a low context culture with a direct communication style. Relationships in both types of culture could be diagrammed like this:

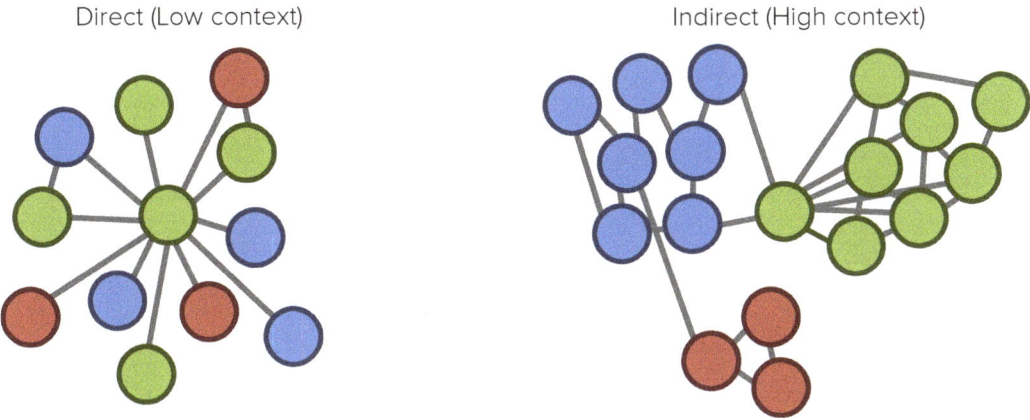

It is important to note that the defining characteristics of cultures are not independent from one another. So cultures that display certain characteristics will also inherently display others that are related. For example, cultures with an individualistic view of self tend to be universalist, low context and use direct communication. A good place to start when trying to understand a culture is to build relationships with local people and to take time to learn from the inside how relationships work.

Associated behaviors

To help you to define more clearly the differences between the direct and indirect styles of communication, we will describe some of the behaviors associated with each.

The following behaviors are commonly associated with **high context, indirect** cultures:

- Communication is like it would be between siblings, where there is a kind of instinctive common understanding.
- People are reluctant to say no because a refusal threatens harmony, which is key in high context cultures.
- You have to read between the lines to understand the real message. What is overtly stated is whatever saves face.
- Use of intermediaries or third parties is frequent, because it avoids direct confrontation.
- Use of understatement is frequent because it is more indirect.
- "Yes" means 'I hear you', not necessarily 'I agree with you'. Where it's difficult to say no, yes has a less definitive meaning.
- People engage in small talk and catching up before getting down to business, because relationships are more important in high context cultures, and small talk cements relationships.
- A seemingly small issue in the context could have a significant meaning in what is being communicated. For example, someone not showing respect by sending an underling to a meeting, or by not providing a refreshment, might mean that all is not well. The message is often not in the words in high context cultures, and these other contextual signals are understood clearly by people in those cultures.
- People are already up to date on what is going on because close-knit networks are common in more collectivist, high context cultures.
- The rank and status of the messenger is as important as the message, because the message is not just in the words.
- People tell you what they think you want to hear so you won't be upset, because face must be saved and outward harmony must be maintained.

The following behaviors are commonly associated with **low context, direct** cultures:

- It's best to tell it like it is, directness is preferred
- It's okay to disagree with your boss at a meeting. To be able to disagree is expected in low context cultures, where people can speak their mind, no matter who they are speaking to.

- "Yes" means 'I agree with you'. Words are taken more literally - on face value - rather than there being other unspoken communication accompanying the meaning of the words.
- Communication is like it would be between two casual acquaintances who have to spell things out because they do not instinctively understand each other.
- It's not necessary to read between the lines, because the meaning is in the words.
- Business is done first, then small talk can take place after the task is completed - if there is time. The task is more important than personal relationships in low context cultures.
- There is rarely any message in the context in low context cultures, so an issue with the context is seen on face value rather than having a significant meaning. For example, someone not providing a refreshment might simply mean they forgot to plan it, rather than that they are trying to tell you they don't want to make a business deal.
- People need to be brought up to date at a meeting because networks are less common, and it would not be expected that everyone had spent time with everyone else.
- The message is what counts, not who the messenger is, because the words carry the meaning, not the context.

Some defining characteristics of direct and indirect cultures

We noted before that the defining characteristics of cultures are not independent and that certain characteristics are related to others. So cultures that tend toward one end of the spectrum in one area will also tend toward that end in other areas too. Below are four continuums representing four areas related to communication - *degree of directness, role of context, importance of face and task or person orientation*. A continuum is a line with opposite views or positions presented at each end. Indirect cultures are represented on the right side of each continuum, and direct cultures on the left.

Degree of Directness

Direct	Indirect
People say what they mean and mean what they say; you don't need to read between the lines; it's important to tell it like it is; honesty is the best policy; the truth is more important than sparing someone's feelings.	People are indirect; they imply or suggest what they mean; understatement is valued; you need to read between the lines; the truth, if it hurts, should be tempered.

STYLES OF COMMUNICATION 1

The Role of Context

Low context	High context
Low context, heterogeneous and individualist cultures; little is already known; the message must be explicit and spelled out; words are the primary means of communication; non-verbal cues are not the key to understanding.	High context, homogenous and collectivist cultures; much is already known; the spoken word is not the primary means of communicating; much is implied but little needs to be said; non-verbal cues and the context are the key; what is not said may be the message.

The importance of Face

Face less important	Face is key
Face has moderate importance; the facts and your purpose are more important than being careful about what you say; getting/giving information is the main goal of the communication exchange; criticism is straightforward; it's okay to say no and to confront people.	Saving face and not losing face take precedence over the facts, maintaining harmony is the main goal of the communication exchange; confrontation is avoided; saying no is difficult; criticism is handled very delicately; what you say and what you feel are often not the same.

The Task or the Person

Task	Person
The task is separated from the person; do business first and then have small talk; establishing a good personal relationship is not essential to getting the job done; the goal is accomplishing the task.	The task and the person can't be separated; begin with small talk and then move to business; personal relationship is a prerequisite to getting the job done; the goal is building the relationship.

Most people who have studied this topic place Australian culture somewhere near the center, but slightly on the direct (low context) side, as in the diagram below:

Direct   Indirect

Swiss   German   American   Australian   Brazilian   African   S. Europe   Arabian   Asian

STYLES OF COMMUNICATION 1

❓ DISCUSSION POINTS

1. What are some of the cultural aspects we have discussed so far that are common in a culture that is a *collectivist* culture? What kind of view of self would be common, what communication style would be prevalent and how would relationships tend to be structured, etc.?

2. Imagine that a Swiss-German person is working on a building project with a Chinese person. Assuming they have a language in common, but considering the differences between their cultures in communication style, what might be some of the communication challenges they could encounter?

3. Think about people that you naturally 'get on with' and those you find more difficult to be around - do you think it has anything to do with differences in communication style?

➡ ACTIVITIES

1. Find five real examples of behaviors associated with the prevalent communication style in your local community. Use the list of behaviors given in this tutorial as a guide, but give real examples that you have seen. In general, do you think your community culture is a *direct* or *indirect* culture in terms of communication style?

2. Watch at least one TV documentary showing people of another culture interacting together. Carefully observe how they communicate with one another, and make a note of any behaviors that point toward their communication style being either direct or indirect.

3. If you have friends from another culture, talk to them about where they fit on the four continuums given at the end of the tutorial. Find out if they have experienced any challenges or misunderstandings related to the area of communication style.

4.11 Styles of communication 2

OBJECTIVES OF THIS TUTORIAL

In this tutorial you will begin by thinking about how to communicate in a more indirect way. Then you will do some exercises to observe non-verbal communication and conversation style.

Introduction

This tutorial assumes that you come from a culture that has a more direct communication style. Because it can be difficult for people from a direct culture to understand and practice indirectness, this tutorial is designed to help you to begin that process.

However, if you come from a culture that has an indirect communication style, you may already have encountered a direct culture and have learned, at least to some degree, how to communicate with people who leave little unspoken. Whatever cultural background you have, if you are intending to live and work in a cross-cultural situation, you need to know your own communication style, and to be willing to practice another style of communication in order to 'speak' clearly to people in your new community.

This tutorial also includes exercises for you to do in your local community - observing and noting different kinds of non-verbal communication. These exercises are helpful for you to begin to get a feel for taking part in and observing real life situations in a deeper, more objective way.

Practicing indirectness

For people who are direct communicators, it can be quite a challenge to say things indirectly - it takes careful thought and patience. Below are seven direct statements, with some suggestions under each one as to how they could be said more indirectly. Read each statement, and before you look at the suggestions, try to rephrase the statement in several different ways to make it more indirect. Then look at the suggestions to see how you did.

While these statements could be appropriate in some situations, imagine that the context here is a formal meeting, where allowing people to save face is important.

1. I don't think that's such a good idea.
    - *Do you think that's a good idea?*
    - *Are there any other ideas?*
    - *I like most parts of that idea.*
2. That's not the point.
    - *That's an interesting point.*
    - *That's another good point.*
    - *Thank you, we seem to be making progress toward the point.*
3. I think we should....
    - *I have one possible suggestion.*
    - *What do you think of this idea?*
    - *I wonder if this might be something to try...*
4. What do you think, Bob?
    - *Does anyone else have any suggestions?*
    - *Have we heard all the opinions?*
5. Those figures are not accurate.
    - *I have some other figures here.*
    - *Those figures may be slightly old.*
    - *I was just given some updated figures.*
6. You're doing that wrong.
    - *I would do that like this.*
    - *Have you tried doing that this way?*
    - *I've done this before, can I help you?*
7. I don't agree.
    - *I have another idea.*
    - *What do you think of this idea?*
    - *May I make a suggestion?*
    - *We might see this slightly differently...*

Decoding indirectness

This exercise is the opposite of the one you just finished. In this activity, the given statements are indirect. You have to explain in direct language what the speaker probably means. Suggestions are given below each statement, but just as in the last exercise, try to rephrase the statement first yourself.

Looking at the first statement, "That is a very interesting viewpoint," remember that the person may mean exactly that, but sometimes it's an indirect way of saying "I disagree with you." In communicating across cultures, you need to at least entertain the possibility that the speaker may mean something other than what he or she has said.

1. That is a very interesting viewpoint.
    - *I don't agree.*
    - *We need to talk more about this.*
    - *You're wrong.*

2. This proposal deserves further consideration.
    - *We don't like it.*
    - *It needs work.*
    - *Propose something else.*

3. I know very little about this, but….
    - *I'm something of an expert on this but am too polite to say so.*
    - *What I think we should do is…*

4. We understand your proposal very well.
    - *Do you have another proposal?*
    - *We don't like it.*

5. We will try our best.
    - *Don't expect much to happen.*
    - *Your project is not our top priority.*

6. I heard another story about that project.
    - *I don't agree with what you said about that project.*
    - *I think you might be exaggerating or trying to 'spin' the truth.*

7. Can we move on to the next topic?
    - *We don't want to talk about this now.*
    - *We need to consult with people not in the room before we can decide.*
    - *Our discussion is not going well on this topic.*

Non-verbal communication

Communication falls into two classic categories: verbal and non-verbal. Non-verbal communication can also be divided into a number of specific subcategories. As you work on this tutorial, you are going to do some practical exercises that will focus on several types of non-verbal communication.

Just like words, gestures, eye contact and other non-verbal cues can have different meanings in different cultures, and they can actually communicate a great deal. It is important to understand them if your goal is to communicate naturally and clearly in another culture. A great place to start is to observe what an important role non-verbal communication has in your own culture, and to take note of all the different forms it takes. The following exercises will help you to do that.

In order to observe non-verbal communication, you will need to hang out in places in your community where you can observe people interacting with one another, like at a church, a shopping center, a restaurant or just around the local streets - take a note book or record audio notes. Your notes from the following exercises will be your assignment to submit for this tutorial.

Gestures

In a number of different settings, watch what people do with their arms, hands, fingers, and whole body. Take notes and try to describe the gestures that you see as "scientifically" as possible *(a man held out his hand, palm down, and wiggled his fingers)* and indicate what you think is the meaning of each gesture *(to call a waiter to his table)*. Take notes on at least four gestures that you observe for each of the following:

1. Arms
2. Hands
3. Fingers
4. Whole body

Eye contact

Observe the degree and nature of eye contact in as many of the following situations as possible and note down what you find for each case:

1. Between two men of the same age
2. Between two women of the same age
3. Between an older and younger man/woman
4. Between a man and woman
5. Between a husband and wife in public
6. Between a boss and employee
7. Between a teacher and a student
8. Between a parent and child
9. Between people passing on the street

Conversational style

Observe the following non-verbal aspects of typical conversations and take note of what you find:

1. How much gesturing goes on in general?
2. How does the transition from one speaker to the next take place? Pick one:
   - speaker A starts before speaker B finishes
   - speaker A starts just after speaker B finishes
   - speaker A pauses before starting
3. How long does one person speak before allowing the other to speak?
4. How do people indicate they want to end the conversation?
5. How do people show disagreement?
6. How do people show displeasure with what they hear?
7. How do people show pleasure at what they are hearing?
8. What is the pattern of eye contact between speaker and listener?

Facial expressions

Observe what people do with their head, eyes, eyebrows, mouth, nose, chin, etc. Record any observations as accurately as you can, indicating what the different facial expressions mean for the following:

1. The Head and Forehead
2. Eyes and Eyebrows

STYLES OF COMMUNICATION 2

3. The Nose
4. The Chin and Jaw
5. Any part of the face or head in combination with the hands and fingers

Personal space

Observe how close various kinds of people stand or sit to each other in various settings:

1. In normal conversation, at work, or on the street
2. In line at the post office, bank, cinema, etc.
3. In an elevator
4. Two men
5. Two women
6. Two children
7. An older and younger person
8. Parent and child
9. A man and woman
10. Husband and wife

Touching

Observe how much and in which parts of the body the following people touch each other:

1. Two men
2. Two women
3. Husband and wife
4. Unrelated man and woman
5. Parent and child
6. Older and younger person

❓ DISCUSSION POINTS

1. How easy did you find it to go out in the community with the purpose of observing the behavior of others - what kind of a challenge is that for you personally? What, if any, responses did you get from people - did you have any conversations with people, or any personal contact during the course of doing the exercises in this tutorial?

2. If people saw you taking notes, what, in your cultural setting, would you say their assumptions might be about what exactly you were doing?

3. Imagine you were doing these same tutorial exercises in a setting where you looked like a 'foreigner' and were new to the culture - what different challenges or advantages do you think you might have?

➡ ACTIVITIES

1. Complete the activities in the tutorial and submit any notes with your assignment. Use the following template for notes (next page). Included are a few examples that might help.

STYLES OF COMMUNICATION 2

Tutorial 4.11 Activity Template

	Gesture	Meaning
1. Arms	*patting someone on the shoulder*	*an expression of friendship or empathy*
2. Hands		
3. Fingers		
4. Whole body		

Eye contact

Note the degree and nature of eye contact between:

1. Two men of the same age - *constant and direct eye contact is maintained throughout the conversation.*
2. Two women of the same age -
3. An older and younger man/woman -
4. A man and woman -
5. A husband and wife in public -
6. A boss and employee -
7. A teacher and a student -

8. A parent and child -

9. People passing on the street -

Conversational style

Notes summarizing your observations of typical conversations in your local community:

1. How much gesturing goes on in general? *Some people use a lot, some use little.*
2. How does the transition from one speaker to the next take place? Pick one:
   - speaker A starts before speaker B finishes
   - speaker A starts just after speaker B finishes
   - speaker A pauses before starting
3. How long does one person speak before allowing the other to speak?
4. How do people indicate they want to end the conversation?
5. How do people show disagreement?
6. How do people show displeasure with what they hear?
7. How do people show pleasure at what they are hearing?
8. What is the pattern of eye contact between speaker and listener?

Facial expressions

	Gesture	Meaning
1. Head and Forehead	*Lowering head and looking pointedly over top of glasses*	*I want to hear more about that, I'm not sure if what you are saying is true*
2. Eyes and Eyebrows		
3. Nose		
4. Chin and Jaw		
5. Any part of the face or head in combination with the hands and fingers		

STYLES OF COMMUNICATION 2

Personal space

How close do people stand or sit in various settings:

1. In normal conversation, at work, or on the street - *Usually one to two meters, generally a lot of personal space is given*
2. In line at the post office, bank, cinema, etc. -
3. In an elevator -
4. Two men -
5. Two women -
6. Two children -
7. An older and younger person -
8. Parent and child -
9. A man and woman -
10. Husband and wife -

Touching

How much and in which parts of the body do the following people touch each other?

1. Two men - *handshake, sometimes a shoulder grab or pat on the shoulder if they are good friends meeting.*
2. Two women -
3. Husband and wife -
4. Unrelated man and woman -
5. Parent and child -
6. Older and younger person -

4.12 The concept of time

OBJECTIVES OF THIS TUTORIAL

This tutorial introduces another of the fundamentals of culture: the concept of time. The two poles of this dimension - *time-oriented* and event/*people oriented* - are defined and explored.

Introduction

Imagine that you are wanting to buy a coffee, and you are walking toward the counter in a small café. But it is busy, and there are four other people converging on the counter at the same time. What would be the right way for you to arrange yourselves in order to get served?

In my culture, we would all try to think about precisely who was first, and in what order the other people came into the shop and approached the counter. Often without any verbal communication, we would make sure that we were all in the correct chronological order and then we would queue up at the counter to be served in that order. If someone obviously skipped ahead in the queue, we would consider that to be "pushing in" and we would feel irritated with the offender - we might even say something about it. Once we are at the counter we would expect the undivided attention of the server until our order was completed.

But on what basis do people in my culture queue for coffee? Queuing or not queuing is a culturally determined behavior based on cultural values. It has quite a bit to do with the value placed on time. Where time is highly valued, a chronological, orderly approach to being served in any setting is the norm. Queuing is an expression of the high value placed on time. Because everyone's time is valuable, whoever arrived first should be served first, and those who arrived later should be served later.

In other cultures the more important factors to consider - other than who arrived first - are things such as who has seniority or who deserves more respect, and maintaining a relationship with all the customers. These cultures place a higher priority on events or people, rather than on time.

Concepts of time

Cultures differ greatly in how people conceive of and handle time, and how their concept of time affects their interactions with each other. The two poles of this dimension - time-oriented and event/people oriented are described below:

Time-oriented

Time is the 'given' - the most important factor - and people are the variable. The needs of people are adjusted to suit the demands of time - schedules, deadlines, etc. Time is quantifiable, and a limited amount of it is available. People do one thing at a time and finish it before starting something else, regardless of circumstances.

Below are some behaviors or characteristics that are more likely to apply to a culture where time is the priority:

- 'Time is money'. Time is given a high value in time-focused cultures.
- To be late is rude. Being 'on time' is important in time-oriented cultures.
- Schedules are sacred, because time depends on schedules.
- The focus is on the task, getting the job done. A time-focus thinks less about people, more about goals.
- Plans are fixed, once agreed upon. Changes in plans upset time-focused people who live by their plans.
- Placing a priority on time is consistent with an individualist viewpoint, because it takes other people into account less than people-focused cultures.
- Having to wait is an insult, because being late is rude in a time-focused culture.
- Interruptions are bad because they upset the schedule.
- People stand in line. Being waited on one at a time is time-focused behavior.

Event/People-oriented

Time is the servant and tool of people. Time is adjusted to suit the needs of people. More time is always available, and you are never too busy. People often have to do several things simultaneously, as required by circumstances. It's not necessary to finish one thing before starting another, nor to finish your business with one person before starting in with another.

Following are some behaviors or characteristics that are more *likely* to apply to a culture where events and people are more important than time:

- Being made to wait is normal and waiting isn't bad in cultures where being on time is less important.

- Interruptions are part of life. Upsetting schedules doesn't matter where schedules aren't that important anyway.
- The focus is on the person and establishing a relationship because people have more value than time.
- Placing a priority on the person is consistent with a collectivist viewpoint, because collectivists are more attuned to the needs of others.
- Deadlines are an approximation because being on time (adhering to deadlines) is not as crucial in a people-focused world.
- To be late is to be late - it doesn't have any other meaning. Being late matters less where time matters less.
- Plans are always changing. When time isn't the priority, plans can change more easily because schedules are not the determining factor.
- People are never too busy to spend time with other people, there is always enough time in a people-focused world.

Below is a diagram of *general tendencies* in regard to time for various cultures, of course generalisations really can't be made, but these are cultural tendencies.

Time is more important / more rigid   Time is less important / less rigid

Swiss   German   American   Japanese   N. Europe   Australian   S. Europe   Chinese   African   Brazilian   Arab

How about you?

The following exercise can help you to discover whether your own behavior tends to be more time-focused or people-focused. It is important to consider where your cultural tendencies lie in regard to this area, particularly if you are considering working with people of another culture, or living in a community that has a different value of time. Being aware that there are widely differing views on the value of time, and what your particular view is, can help you to avoid misunderstandings and frustration. Knowing your own point of view and seeing it from the other person's point of view is a big step to becoming a part of your new community.

After reading the paired statements below (a. and b.), choose the one that best describes the action you would take or the way you feel about the particular topic.

    1a. People should stand in line so they can be waited on one at a time.

    1b. There's no need to stand in line - people will be waited on when they are ready.

THE CONCEPT OF TIME

2a. Interruptions should be avoided wherever possible.

2b. Interruptions usually cannot be avoided and are often quite beneficial.

3a. It's more efficient if you do one thing at a time.

3b. I can get as much done if I work on two or three things at the same time.

4a. It's more important to stick to the schedule.

4b. It's more important to complete the task, transaction, or conversation.

5a. Unanticipated events are hard to accommodate and should be avoided where possible.

5b. Unexpected things happen all the time; that's life.

6a. You shouldn't take a telephone call or acknowledge a visitor when you are meeting with another person.

6b. It would be rude not to take a phone call if I'm in, or to ignore a visitor who drops by.

7a. Deadlines are like a promise; many other things depend on them, so they should not be treated lightly.

7b. You shouldn't take deadlines too seriously; anything can happen. What's a deadline between friends?

8a. It's important, in a meeting or a conversation, not to become distracted or digress. You should stick to the agenda.

8b. Digressions, distractions are inevitable. An agenda is just a piece of paper.

9a. I tend to be task-oriented.

9b. I tend to be people-oriented.

10a. Personal talk should be saved for after hours or during lunch.

10b. Personal talk is part of the job.

Now that you have made your selections, calculate whether you came out more on the time- or event/people-oriented side. The behaviors listed under 'a' tend to be more characteristic of time-focused people. The behaviors listed under 'b' tend to be more characteristic of event/people-focused people. Keep in mind that there is nothing scientific about this exercise, that it doesn't prove anything about you. But it might give you some idea of your own tendencies and some food for thought as to how you might relate in another cultural context.

❓ DISCUSSION POINTS

1. Some analysts today say that younger people - those under 40 - in Western cultures are tending toward being less rigid with time. They say this is because older generations were not exposed to the mass media of today where multi-tasking and moving from one thing to another is common-place. Do you agree with this, and if so what evidence or examples can you give?

2. What specific challenges in the area of time do you think would face someone from Germany moving to the Arab world to do business?

➡ ACTIVITIES

1. Try to find as many examples as you can in the real world of time-focused or event/people-focused behaviors, as you go about your life this week. List the behaviors you noted and describe how they illustrate the underlying value of time.

2. When living in a cross-cultural community, it is often necessary for people to change their schedule to fit in to their new community and to be able to spend more time with local people. Choose two of your normal activities and for one week, change the time that you do them, for example:

- have your evening meal an hour earlier or an hour later than normal,
- take a walk around your community when your favorite TV show is on,
- wash your laundry at a laundromat rather than at home,
- buy meat, vegetables and bread from small stores rather than at the supermarket,
- visit a neighbor or friend, or go out for a meal with them, at a time when you would normally be at home.

4.13 Culture in the workplace

OBJECTIVES OF THIS TUTORIAL

This tutorial examines the impact of cultural differences that occur when people are working together - specifically differences in *concepts of power, attitudes to uncertainty* and *the concept of status*.

Introduction

Culture comes into sharpest focus in human interactions, and one of the greatest arenas for such interaction is when people are working together. So, in this tutorial are going to examine the impact of culture on a variety of work-related behaviors and the underlying values associated with those behaviors. We will look at three dimensions of cultural difference that have particular implications for the workplace:

- The *concept of power*.
- The *attitude toward uncertainty and the unknown*.
- The *concept of the source of status*.

The concept of power: high and low power- distance

The attitude of a society toward inequality, or how cultures deal with people's different levels of status and their access to power, is referred to as *power-distance*. Power-distance is especially evident when people are working together, particularly in the role and relationship of the person 'in charge' and their subordinates. Here are brief descriptions of the two poles of this concept, high and low power-distance:

High power-distance

People in these cultures accept that inequalities in power and status are natural or existential. In the same way they accept that some people are smarter than others, people accept that some will have more power and influence than others. Those with power tend to emphasize it, to hold it close and not delegate or share it, and to distinguish themselves as much as possible from those who do not have power. They are, however, expected to accept the responsibilities that go with power, to look after those beneath them. Subordinates are not expected to take any initiative and are closely supervised.

Below is a list of characteristics and behaviors that reflect an attitude of high power-distance.

- People are less likely to question the boss because there is more fear of displeasing the boss in high power distance cultures.
- Elitism is the norm. Because it is normal to emphasize distinctions between the boss and subordinates.
- Those in power have special privileges in high power-distance cultures.
- There are greater wage differences between managers and subordinates.
- Workers prefer precise instructions from superiors and close supervision, the visible exercise of power, is common to these cultures.
- Bosses are independent; subordinates are dependent. There is an unequal distribution of power.
- Freedom of thought could get you into trouble and independence is not valued in subordinates.
- Less social mobility is the norm, which keeps those with and without power separated.
- The chain of command is sacred because rank must be respected; you should not 'go around' people.
- The pecking order is clearly established, there is a need to show who has power over whom.
- Management style is authoritarian and paternalistic. Bosses are supposed to wield their power.
- Interaction between boss and subordinate is formal, which emphasizes the power gap.

Low power-distance

People in these cultures see inequalities in power and status as largely artificial: it is not natural, though it may be convenient, that some people have power over others. Those with power, therefore, tend to de-emphasize it, to minimize the differences between themselves and their subordinates, and to delegate and share power as much as possible. Subordinates are rewarded for taking the initiative and do not like close supervision.

Below is a list of characteristics and behaviors that reflect an attitude of low power-distance.

- Students question teachers because superiors do not have to be deferred to.
- Freedom of thought is encouraged and no one is threatened by independence or thinking for oneself.
- The chain of command is mainly for convenience, power differences are not emphasized.
- Interaction between boss and subordinate is more informal because the distance is minimized.
- Subordinates and bosses are interdependent. 'We're all equal here so we all depend on each other'.
- It's okay to question the boss because he's just another worker.
- Management style is consultative and democratic because 'We are all in this together', power distance is de-emphasized.

Working with power-distance differences

Cultural misunderstandings can occur when people from a low-power distance culture and a high-power distance culture work together. This could be in any environment where people are working together, including a church or religious group, a community group, an office or business, or when working with government or local officials.

Because power distinctions are not recognized in the same way, probably the most commonly occurring misunderstanding is that a person from a low power-distance culture can inadvertently communicate a lack of respect for the person or authority of those "in power" in a high power-distance culture. It can cause tension and relationship problems when low power-distance working practice is applied in the high power-distance work environment, for example:

- *Questioning the boss* - In low power-distance cultures it is normal practice to ask the boss for some clarification or to give input into a decision that has been made. But in many high power-distance cultures, bosses are not used to having their decisions questioned or, worse, having to explain them to subordinates. In these cultures, bosses make decisions, and subordinates carry them out. And if there are questions, they would normally be raised in a very delicate way and always through the proper channels. This doesn't mean bosses are unapproachable or infallible, but you do have to think long and hard before challenging those in power, and then do so in the appropriate way.

- *Taking initiative without asking the boss first* - In many low power-distance cultures it is a good thing to see something that needs to be done and just do it, without waiting to be told. In high power-distance cultures, that kind of behavior is often interpreted as taking power that hasn't been given to you. You have made a decision that wasn't yours to make, and in the process usurped and threatened the authority of the person who is supposed to make such a decision. In cultures where power is highly centralized and closely guarded, taking initiative is a risky business.

- *Being too informal with those in power* - In high power-distance cultures, interaction between the higher ranks and the lower ranks, or any mixing of the ranks, is relatively uncommon and tends to be quite formal. People in power don't just spend social time with their subordinates on the spur of the moment; most people in that situation would feel quite uncomfortable and awkward. In these cultures, people of higher status tend not to regard themselves as being like workers, nor do they want to be seen that way. The greater the gulf between the higher ranks and the lower echelons, the better for everyone.

- *Bypassing the chain of command* - In many cultures, bypassing the chain of command will not be appreciated. The proper thing to do would be to discuss an issue with the person directly above you in the chain of command, not to go directly to a higher boss. If the one above you doesn't respond, then you could either announce that you are going to talk to the boss or ask the one directly above you to do so. If he still does nothing, then you can go to the higher boss with relative impunity, having gone through the proper channels.

People from low power-distance cultures can find the formality, lack of independence and the more authoritarian management style frustrating to work with as it can seem inefficient and counter-productive. Conversely, people from high power-distance cultures can find people from low power-distance cultures disrespectful, pushy, threatening, and disruptive of the working harmony.

If you are working cross-culturally, it is important to take time to get to know your new community or coworkers, and *how* they work together - don't just assume that you know how to work in another culture without a time of learning first. It is very helpful to take a back seat in the beginning - to observe and learn with an open mind and a positive attitude. Don't try to jump in and improve things or change things in the early days, but take time to learn how things work first. Recognize the fact that things do get done and that the society does work, but that things get done differently to what you are used to. Eventually, if you go carefully and learn as you go, you will find that you become more like the local people and are able to fit in and to work well with them.

Attitude toward uncertainty and the unknown: high and low uncertainty avoidance

Another dimension of culture that particularly affects the workplace is how people respond to the inherent uncertainty of life. This uncertainty creates anxiety in all cultures, with characteristic responses - technology to control uncertainty in the natural world; laws, regulations, and procedures to control the uncertainty in human behavior; and religious rituals to address people's spiritual uncertainty.

While all societies feel threatened by uncertainty, some feel more threatened by it than others do. Depending on their attitudes, different cultures have developed different ways of dealing with it. The two extremes, called *high uncertainty avoidance and low uncertainty avoidance*, are described below:

High uncertainty avoidance

Cultures characterized by high uncertainty avoidance feel especially anxious about the uncertainty in life and try to limit and control it as much as possible. They have more laws, regulations, policies, and procedures and a greater emphasis on obeying them. They also have a strong tendency toward conformity, hence predictability. People take comfort in structure, systems, and expertise - anything that can blunt or even neutralize the impact of the unexpected. The unknown is frightening.

These behaviors are more commonly associated with high uncertainty avoidance cultures:

- Punctuality is highly valued because sticking to the schedule is comforting.
- People should keep emotions under control, because when people lose control of emotions, anything can happen!
- 'Different' is dangerous, because it is unpredictable or unknown.
- People expect more formality in interactions because that assures a certain order in the unfolding of interactions.
- The chain of command should never be bypassed - going around the structure threatens its very survival, and where would we be without structure?
- People believe less in 'common sense' - they are more likely to listen to people with expertise; the common person couldn't know that much.
- Conflict in organizations should be eliminated as it threatens the smooth running of things.
- People change jobs infrequently because stability is sought and provided for; change is threatening.

- A general sense of anxiety prevails because of the fear of the unknown.
- People accept authority more readily; authority is comforting because it guarantees order and keeps things under control.
- Rules should not be broken - they are the foundation of order.
- Risks should be avoided - they are inherently unsettling because they involve the unknown.

Low uncertainty avoidance

People in these cultures do not feel quite so threatened nor anxious about uncertainty, and therefore do not have such a strong need to limit or control it. They seek to legislate fewer areas of human interaction and tolerate differences better. They feel boxed in by too much structure or too many systems. They are curious rather than frightened by the unknown and are not uncomfortable leaving things to chance. Life is interesting but not especially daunting.

These behaviors are more commonly associated with low uncertainty avoidance cultures:

- People change jobs with more frequency because change is not so frightening.
- People more readily accept dissent because differing views are nothing to be afraid of; nothing is set in stone.
- Take things one day at a time, you can't know or control the future anyway.
- People should let their emotions out, there's nothing to fear from emotions.
- Conflict in organizations is natural and nothing to be afraid of. Order doesn't break down or get undermined that easily.
- Differences are interesting - the unknown is not frightening.
- A general sense of well-being prevails and there isn't that much fear of what can't be understood or controlled.
- People accept authority less readily; authority is limiting and control is not that comforting.
- Rules can be broken if it makes sense, for pragmatic reasons. Rules can be limiting; there's nothing inherently satisfying about rules.
- Risks are opportunities, since the unknown isn't particularly worrying, risks are not to be feared.

This area of culture, just as with power-distance, can cause tension in the workplace where people with different views are trying to work together. It will help you greatly if you face conflict or issues when working with people of another culture, to consider whether differences in uncertainty avoidance or another deeper cultural attitude may be a root cause. Remember to ask local friends for advice - tell them you are still learning how to relate and that you need their help. If you make a mistake, don't worry too much, explain, apologize and then move on.

The source of status - achieved or ascribed

Another work-related cultural area to think about is how people come by their status - in their organizations, and in society in general. This concept is related to power-distance in some ways and also to individualism/collectivism. The two poles of this concept are sometimes referred to as *achieved status* and *ascribed status*, or as *doing* cultures and *being* cultures. They are briefly described below.

Achieved status ('doing' cultures)

In these *doing* cultures, people are looked up to and respected because of their personal and especially their professional accomplishments. You get ahead into positions of power and influence by virtue of your achievements and performance. Your status is earned and not merely a result of birth, age, or seniority. You are hired based on your record of success, not on the basis of family background, connections, or the school you attended. People aren't particularly impressed with titles. Education is important, but not the mere fact of it: you have to have done something with your knowledge. Status is not automatic and can be lost if you stop achieving.

Ascribed status ('being' cultures)

In these *being* cultures, a certain amount of status is built into the person; it is automatic and therefore difficult to lose. You are looked up to because of the family and social class you are born into, because of your affiliations and membership in certain important groups, and, later, because of your age and seniority. The school you went to and the amount of education you received also confer status, whether or not you did well in school or have done anything with your education. Titles are important and should always be used. You are pressured to justify the power, respect and deference that you automatically enjoy. You cannot lose your status completely, but you can lose respect by not realizing your potential.

CULTURE IN THE WORKPLACE

? DISCUSSION POINTS

1. Discuss the two following incidents which have come about in part because of cultural differences involving status. Think about what you would do in each situation.

Sitting down or standing up?

You are teaching English in an Asian country. When you enter the classroom, all your students automatically stand up until you give them the signal to sit. You are uncomfortable with this deferential behavior and tell your students they don't need to stand when you enter the room.

After two weeks, the headmaster tells you that the other teachers are upset with you because they have heard that your students don't stand when you enter the room. They think the students are showing disrespect, and are worried it could spread to their classrooms. They also think that you are trying to be popular by deliberately blurring the distinction between teacher and student (and if students put themselves on the same level as teachers, chaos will result). What would you do about the teachers' reactions?

Back of the bus

You have a job working for the local government in another country. Every morning a bus carrying laborers to work stops at your house to give you a ride to work. Your boss, a department manager, and a second professional always sit up front together, but you like to sit in the back and talk with the laborers. After a few days, your boss says you are confusing the workers with your informal behavior and warns you that you will lose their respect if you don't start acting like a professional. How do you respond?

➡ ACTIVITIES

1. For each of the continuums listed on the following page (which are all cultural areas related to working), identify the point on the spectrum that you think best represents your own behavior.

Tutorial 4.13 Activity Sheet

Concept of Work

Work As Part Of Identity	Work As Functional Necessity
Work has value in and of itself. Your job is an important part of your identity. People live to work, in the sense that getting things done is inherently satisfying.	Work is the means to paying bills and meeting financial obligations. It may be satisfying but doesn't have to be. Life is too short to revolve around one's work. Work is what I do, not who I am.

Motivation

Professional Opportunity	Comfortable Work Environment
Professional opportunity and success are important motivating factors. People want to learn, get ahead, move up in their professions or organizations and have greater power, authority and responsibility. Job security is not so important as the chance to make more money and advance in one's career.	People are motivated by the desire to have a pleasant work setting and good relationships with co-workers. Job security is important, as is an organization that takes care of its employees. Having more time off to spend with family is also very motivating. More power and responsibility are not of themselves attractive, even if they mean more money.

Personal and Professional

Personal/Professional Separated	Personal/Professional Intertwined
Personal matters should not be brought to work. Personal/family obligations should be scheduled around work. The personal and professional lives should and can be kept separate. The human factor is real but can't be indulged in the workplace. People won't understand if you plead a family emergency.	It is impossible to separate personal and family matters from work. You may have to interrupt work to take care of personal business. The personal and professional lives inevitably overlap. People will understand if you plead a family emergency.

The Key to Productivity

Results	Harmony
Focusing on the task ensures success. People won't always get along, but you have to move forward anyway. Harmony is nice but results are what count. If you get results, people will be more harmonious. Getting results is ultimately more important than how you get them.	Working well with other people is the key to success in any enterprise. Harmony in the workplace will ensure eventual success. Getting things done hinges on people getting along well. Results bought at the expense of harmony are too costly. How you get results is just as important as the results themselves.

The Ideal Worker

Technical Skills	People Skills
What matters most in a worker is his/her technical qualifications: education, work experience, and specific skills. "People" skills are important, but they don't contribute as much to the bottom line. Hiring a relative would be sheer coincidence and only if he/she had the skills you needed. Demonstrated competence is the key to getting promoted.	What matters most in a worker is his/her ability to work well with others and not rock the boat. Experience and technical skills are important, but they don't contribute as much to the bottom line. Hiring a relative is always a good bet. Age and seniority are important for getting promoted.

It is interesting to note that the mark indicating the more global, Western cultural position is normally on the left side on all of these continuums. People from other cultures (that tend more toward the right) often categorize people from a Western culture in the following ways:

- *Power-distance:* They don't respect bosses very much. Or bosses are entirely too chummy with subordinates.
- *Uncertainty avoidance:* They take too many risks and don't respect traditions enough.
- *Source of status*: Achievements matter too much to them. They don't believe in the wisdom of experience or the significance of one's social class and upbringing.

- *Concept of work:* They can't enjoy life because work and success matter too much to them.
- *Motivation:* They think too much about the professional side of work and life; they should worry more about the human side. They want to get ahead, but for what? We all die, even those who are ahead.
- *Personal/professional:* They try to separate life into artificial boxes. It's not as black and white as they think. Life is grey.
- *Key to productivity:* They are too fixated on output and results, the 'what'; they aren't concerned enough about the 'how'. They don't realize the 'how' affects the 'what'.
- *Ideal worker:* Anybody can have skills (or get them); what matters is personal qualities. Westerners focus on the superficial, what the person can do; they should focus on the substance, on who the person is.

4.14 Control: Who is in charge?

OBJECTIVES OF THIS TUTORIAL

This tutorial introduces another fundamental area of culture: the *locus of control* - which is the extent to which individuals believe that they can control the events that affect them. We will define and explore the two poles of this dimension; activism and fatalism.

Introduction

Which of the following two statements do you most agree with?

a. What happens to me is my own doing.

b. Sometimes I feel I don't have control over the direction my life is taking.

When asked the same question, the percentage of Americans who chose A was 89%, but the percentage of Chinese who chose A was only 35%.

Why is there such a great difference between the American and Chinese percentages? There could be many explanations, but one almost certainly is the fact that many Americans believe in the power of the individual to prevail against all obstacles, that there is nothing people cannot do, or become, if they want it badly enough and are willing to make the effort: "Where there is a will there is a way." Conversely, if people are not doing well, Americans tend to think it is the individual who is to blame. The American view is *activism*, the view that the locus of control is *internal*.

In Chinese culture, many people believe that while you can shape your life to some extent, certain external forces, things beyond your control, also play an important part. They say that what happens to you in life is not entirely in your hands. The Chinese view is *fatalism*, the view that the locus of control is *external*.

Locus of control - internal or external

Cultures differ greatly in their view of a person's place in the external world, especially the degree to which human beings can control or manipulate forces outside themselves and shape their own destiny. The two sides of this dimension, internal and external control, are described below:

Internal (activism)

The locus of control is largely internal, within the individual. There are very few givens in life, few circumstances that have to be accepted as they are, that cannot be changed. There are no limits on what I can do or become, so long as I set my mind to it and make the necessary effort. Life is what I *do*.

The following sets of statements are characteristic of a view that the locus of control is internal:

- The laws of the universe can be discovered.
- Progress is inevitable, as people figure out more and more about the world.
- Every problem has a solution. If the world is a mechanism, then it's possible to know how it works; no problem should be unsolvable if you look hard enough.
- Optimism is the rule because humans are in control.
- Where there's a will there's a way.
- People believe strongly in technology. Mechanisms (technology) are a hallmark of internally controlled thinking.
- Unhappiness is your own fault.
- You make your own luck.

External (fatalism)

The locus of control is largely external to the individual. Some aspects of life are predetermined, built into the nature of things. There are limits beyond which we cannot go and certain givens that cannot be changed and must be accepted. Life is largely what *happens* to me.

The following sets of statements are characteristic of a view that the locus of control is external:

- Stoicism is the rule.
- Some things are a matter of luck or chance.
- Progress is not automatic because anything can happen.
- The workings of the universe are ultimately unknowable.
- Nature cannot be dominated by man.
- Some problems do not have solutions - not everything is knowable.
- Where there's a will there's a will - you can't necessarily make things happen.

- Unhappiness is a natural part of life and you can't always be happy because that would mean you were in control.

What about you? Internal and external control

Below are a number of paired statements (a. and b.). Immediately after reading each pair, write down the letter of the one of the two that best describes the action you would take or the way you feel about the particular topic. Then see whether you came out more on the internal or external control side.

1a. If I'm unhappy, I should do something about it.

1b. Nothing's broken if I'm unhappy; it's just part of life's ups and downs.

2a. The external world is a mechanism like other mechanisms; its workings can be discovered, predicted, even manipulated.

2b. The external world is complex, dynamic and organic. It cannot ultimately be known.

3a. It is important to have a positive attitude about life.

3b. You should see life as it really is.

4a. If I try hard enough and want something bad enough, nothing can stop me from getting what I want.

4b. Some things are beyond my reach, no matter what I do.

5a. What is new is usually better.

5b. What is new is suspect.

6a. I make my own luck.

6b. Many things happen because of chance or luck.

7a. Every problem has a solution, if you look hard enough.

7b. Some problems don't have a solution.

8a. I tend to be proactive and a doer.

8b. I tend to be stoic.

9a. If a friend is depressed, I would try to cheer him/her up.

9b. If a friend is depressed, there is no need for me to do anything.

The "a" statements tend to be more characteristic of internally controlled people. The "b" statements tend to be more characteristic of externally controlled people.

Australia - a fatalist nation?

Thomas Hartmann, in his blog 'Four Cultures' wrote the following piece about Australian culture. He explores the idea that fatalism is active, not passive. If you come from a different culture, think about how the idea of the locus of control exhibits itself in your home culture.

Fatal Nation

The prime example of a society dominated by a fatalist activism is Australia. I'm hardly the first to notice this. The Fatal Shore (Hughes 1987) and The Lucky Country (Horne 1964) are two epithets that have stuck. Its modern foundation as an archipelago of repressive penal colonies, its history of near genocidal oppression of the indigenous population, together with its genuinely unpredictable climate (dominated by El Nino Southern Oscillation) make this a continent uniquely conditioned by and for fatalism. Australia has 1 gaming machine for every 99 people (contrasting with the UK at one per 236 people or the US at one per 426, according to the 2004 World Count of Gaming Machines). These produce significant revenue for the government, particularly in NSW, strongly impacting on policy. Policing is controlled by fatalism. A widespread Government advert says 'More police: more chance of getting caught'. Every social event includes a raffle; even the recent Monet exhibition at the Gallery of NSW ended with online competition entry to win a trip to Giverny. These are all examples of contrived randomness hard at work every day. To sum up: at least one country is in constant danger of suffering a monoculture of fatalism. Meanwhile, cultural theorists themselves conspire to create a limited culture that mistakenly regards fatalism as inactive, and therefore irrelevant.

❓ DISCUSSION POINTS

1. One of the most common complaints of people from Western cultures working around the world is how long it takes to "get things done" in their host country. Sometimes the complaint appears in comments about the slow pace of life overseas. This Western urge to 'do something', is sometimes inconsistent with one of the goals of cross-cultural work which is to encourage other people to get involved. How do you think you'll be able to deal with this situation, to reconcile the activist side of your character (if you are an activist)? Will you have to redefine your idea of accomplishment or of success?

2. How do you think cultural conditioning concerning the locus of control effects the ability of believers from different cultures to trust in God to meet their needs?

3. Do you think a person's view of the locus of control is a spiritual concept or a cultural concept, or both?

➡ ACTIVITIES

1. Try to find a friend from a different culture who is willing to take the self-test (the numbered statements in the tutorial) on internal or external control. Explain to them that you are learning about cultural differences. Read each pair of statements to them and have them pick the one that they agree with. Make a report on your findings, specifically any differences you see between their view and your view.

2. Write a short response to Thomas Hartmann's blog piece on Australia as a fatalist nation. If you are from another culture, write some notes about how the view of the locus of control exhibits itself in your culture.

4.15 Social relationships

OBJECTIVES OF THIS TUTORIAL

This tutorial begins to look at relationships - what they look like, what they are based on, and how they vary across cultures.

Introduction

In a sense, your entire life is nothing but a series of relationships with all kinds of people in a wide variety of roles. The things you are learning about culture and cultural differences are only going to be meaningful when applied in specific situations with specific individuals - as you handle relationships - both social and work-related.

The circle of relationships

As you enter the world of social relationships in a new community, you will need to develop a good understanding of how people usually relate to one another. That will take time, as you interact and learn from the people in your new community. First, however you need to learn how relationships work on a bigger level in your own community. This exercise asks you to construct a map or chart for yourself for your own setting, showing how you relate to, and regard other people.

Below is a list of types of people, and a diagram with a series of rings or concentric circles with you in the center. Draw your own circle diagram on a piece of paper, then write each type of person in one of the rings, nearer to or further from the center depending on any or all of the following criteria:

- how closely you are involved in that person's life and vice versa;
- how responsible you feel for the happiness and well-being of that person and vice versa;
- how much of your inner life, your most private thoughts and feelings, you share with that person and vice versa;
- how much that person "means" to you.

SOCIAL RELATIONSHIPS

You can add other types of people and leave off any on the list that don't apply to you. Add to the rings if necessary or to draw your own chart if the placement of the rings doesn't suit you. Don't worry about being too precise: the idea is to get a general sense of the personal and emotional closeness you feel toward the people in your life.

- Your parents
- Complete strangers
- People you've met once or twice
- Your brother(s)
- Acquaintances
- Good friends
- Your spouse
- Your sister(s)
- Your grandparents
- Your first cousins
- Your closest friends
- Your aunts and uncles
- Your second cousins
- Your children
- Your boss
- Your in-laws

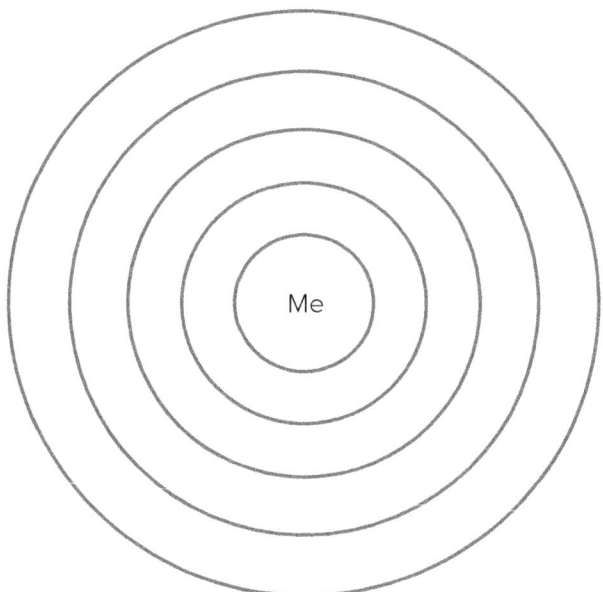

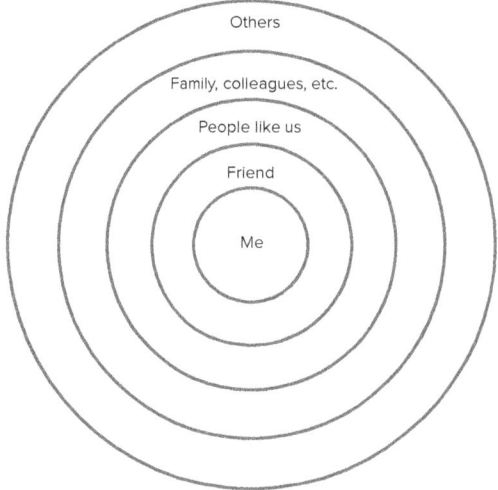

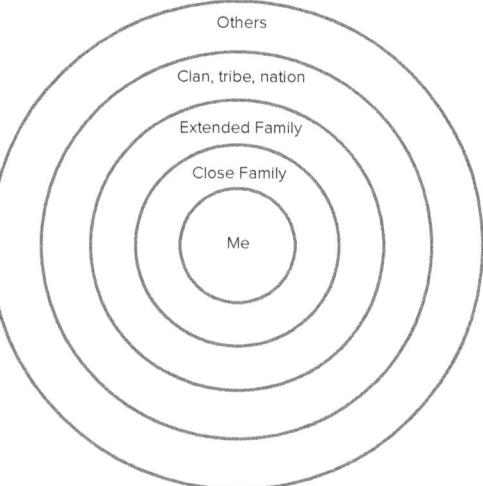

When you have finished, compare your chart with the ones below, which are examples of how people from different cultural backgrounds would organise the general categories of people in their personal relationship chart.

The first diagram could be from a Western individualist culture, where friends are just as important as family (or more so). The second diagram is from a collectivist culture, where family and group ties determine personal and social closeness, and friendships with others are not considered to be nearly as important.

The fact is that emotional and social distance from other people is greatly affected by culture. For example, the African idea of 'family' is large. Cousins and second cousins all fall under the heading of brother or sister, and uncles and aunts function as parents. If I was a student and wanted to study in Dakar, the assumption would be that I could live in the city with my extended family. This would also be true in many Asian cultures.

It can be very helpful for you to understand how people think about their "circle of relationships" when you are entering into relationships with people from another culture. You may make a "friend" in another culture, but what does friendship mean to that person, and is their assumption of their relationship with you the same as your own assumption?

Social Relationships - making friends

It is important to learn how to develop new friendships in your own culture to be better prepared for trying to make friends in another culture. Most people just let friendships 'happen to them' without actively seeking them out - this might be OK in your own setting and culture, but when you move to a new town, new area or a new country you will have to become actively thoughtful about making friends in order to become a part of the new community.

Relationships always begin as superficial acquaintances and then in some cases progress to deep friendships. So, if your goal is ultimately to form friendships, you must start out at the surface level and from there you may eventually form a deeper friendship. Recall how your previous good friendships have started. They weren't profound at the beginning. They were superficial. And you gradually got to know your friends better. You shared more experiences. You found more common ground as time went on. You began to trust one another. That's how it works. You can't skip the superficial stage, so you might as well master that level first.

Many of the friendships you formed in childhood began before you even remember. But this is how they began. This is how they all start: first you learn a person's name and where they are from and what they do what they do for a living, or where they go to school, etc. Then you learn their interests. If you find common ground, the relationship gradually moves from the superficial to the deeper and more lasting kind of friendship.

SOCIAL RELATIONSHIPS

How do people make friends?

What are some of the ways that friendships are typically formed in our culture? Some suggestions (feel free to add your own suggestions to this list):

- Many people make friends at work. Open yourself up to the possibilities by participating in social occasions, such as dinners or lunches to celebrate birthdays.
- Follow your interests. For example, join a neighborhood walking group or sporting team, a Bible study or a painting class.
- If you don't work and have no particular hobbies, consider joining a volunteer group with a charity that interests you.
- Use your existing network of family and friends to meet new people.
- When you have the opportunity to be friendly - at work, at church, any time - make an effort to be friendly and interested in other people.
- Don't turn down social invitations, see them as opportunities to meet people and develop deeper relationships.
- Invite people out for a coffee or over to your home.

When making friends is difficult

Many people find it difficult to make friends. They might be shy, or feel they lack the social skills to start a conversation. Suggestions include:

- Join groups that share your common interests. Talking about one of your interests, such as gardening or writing short stories, for example, will be easier for you and can help give you confidence to talk about other things with potential new friends.
- Watch and learn from gregarious people who make friends easily. If you know someone like this well, why not ask them for some 'conversation tips' or advice.
- Practice looking people in the eye when you talk to them.
- Listen to what others are saying, rather than focusing on your own self-consciousness or your own interests.
- Actively listen and prepare a "follow-up" question to ask about what the person just said - try to get them talking about things that interest them.
- Smile.
- Look for anyone else in the room who seems socially awkward, and approach them for conversation.
- When you talk to someone new, ask them simple questions about themselves or what they like to do; it's a good way to get started.

- Social skills *can* be learned, and the more you step out of your comfort zone and try, the easier it will be next time - so never give up.

Romantic relationships

The dynamics of romantic relationships are often puzzling enough in your own culture, but even more complicated in an intercultural context. The reason we are covering it here, is that norms for romantic relationships are influenced by culture: different cultures give signals in different ways. You may be the object of someone else's interest or you may unintentionally communicate interest in another person, who then responds. It is important, then, for you to be aware of any differences between the norms governing romantic relationships in your own culture and to be aware that those in another culture may be different and may also be very subtle. This is something you will learn through time spent with people in your new community.

Think about the questions below and how you would answer them from the perspective of your own culture. Feel free to add any other questions of your own.

1. How does a man show he is interested in a woman?
2. How does a woman show she is interested in a man?
3. How does a man show he is not interested in a woman who is interested in him?
4. How does a woman show she is not interested in a man who is interested in her?
5. How do you know when the relationship is becoming something more than just friendship? What are signs that the other person is taking this relationship much more seriously?
6. What do men/women do to show they want to pull back on or cool down the relationship?
7. How much touching, embracing, and kissing is appropriate for a couple in public?

Read the incident below and think about what might have contributed to the misunderstandings that occurred.

Wedding bells

Angela (an Australian working in India) is an outgoing, vivacious, and warm person with a ready smile. She introduces herself to people at social events and makes them feel at ease. Last week, a shy, middle-aged widower at work asked her out to dinner, and she accepted and had a pleasant evening. He asked her again this week, and while she was somewhat hesitant, she accepted again. Now, today, he has sent her a beautiful card - containing a marriage proposal. Angela, by the way, is 24 and not interested in marriage. Now what?

What signals did Angela give that might have been misinterpreted, or what foundational cultural understandings might have been different to begin with?

SOCIAL RELATIONSHIPS

? DISCUSSION POINTS

1. The following is how a number of Australian young people responded when asked "What makes a good friend?" (source: reachout.com)

- someone who will support you no matter what
- someone you can trust and who won't judge you
- someone who won't put you down or deliberately hurt your feelings, but will show kindness and respect
- someone who will love you not because they feel they have to because you're their friend, but because they choose to
- someone whose company you enjoy and whose loyalty you can depend upon
- someone who will be there no matter what your situation is
- someone who is trustworthy and not afraid to tell you the truth, no matter how hard it is sometimes
- someone who can laugh when you laugh
- someone who will stick around when things get rough
- someone who makes you smile
- someone who can accept you for who you are, and just lend you an ear when you need to whine or complain
- someone who will cry when you cry
- someone who will give you room to change.

Think about the types of things that they have included and if you agree with all the points in this description. What, if anything, would you add to the list or take out of it?

2. This exercise focuses on one key aspect of friendship: the responsibilities or obligations it incurs. If the requests below were put to you by a very close friend - someone who you would place in an inner circle on the relationship diagram - what would your answer be? For each question below think about whether you would answer "yes" or "no".

- Would you lend this person a substantial amount of money?
- Would you lie for this person in a situation where he/she was in trouble?

- Would you use your position or influence to help this person gain a special advantage over other people in getting a job in your organization?
- Would you serve as a go-between for this person in a difficult work situation?
- Would you let this person copy from your paper on an exam?
- Would you intervene in a family or marital dispute if this person asked you to?
- Would you agree to take care of this friend's child for an extended period during a family/personal emergency?
- Would you look after this friend's house while he/she was away?
- Would you give a positive recommendation for this person if you did not think he/she would be good in a particular job?
- Would you help this person do something illegal if he/she asked you to?

➡ ACTIVITIES

1. Make a list of the types of places you typically visit during the course of your normal life where you might be likely to meet new people. Now make another list of the types of activities you could add to your routine in order to put yourself into proximity with more new people if your goal was to meet as many new people in your community as possible.

2. During the coming weeks, actively try to meet and have conversations with people you have never met before - practicing being friendly, asking questions and finding out about their life and interests.

4.16 Culture/Language acquisition 1

OBJECTIVES OF THIS TUTORIAL

This tutorial introduces Culture/Language acquisition. It looks at how your purpose and long term goals of learning another culture and language should change the way in which you learn.

Introduction

There are many language learning programs available today, especially if you plan to learn one of the major languages of the world. So when you consider second language acquisition, you could potentially choose from any of the following types of language courses:

- General courses based on language structure (grammar)
- Reading, writing and vocabulary courses
- Speaking and listening courses
- Intensive courses offered by language schools
- Short-term immersion courses
- Software courses
- Classroom or university programs
- Language for specific professions (medical, business, law, teaching, etc.)
- Courses for academic purposes
- Courses for children
- Courses for over 50s
- One-to-one courses
- Online or video courses

So how should someone decide which kind of language learning program is the best one for them? Before you decide *how* to learn a language you should first think about *why* you are learning it - what are your long-term goals?

Long term goals

Imagine that someone had the long-term goal of planting a church in a community with a different language and culture to their own. They might draw a timeline for the next five or so years of their life that would look something like this:

| Move in | Language Learning | Evangelism | Teaching & Discipleship |

This focus on their own *personal tasks* would be a very typical way for a person to begin to think and make a plan for such a long and complex process as planting a church cross-culturally. After deciding that the end goal is "me being able to minister in the community", then they might move on to think more specifically about "the things I need to do" or "the steps I need to take" in order to reach that goal. For some large undertakings this may be the best way to go about things, such as building a house for example where a list of tasks would be a help in bringing the project to completion - but not surprisingly, church planting is different to building a house. Why? Because church planting is something that is done in partnership with God and it is essentially about Him communicating Himself to people through other people - so from the very beginning those people and the way they understand things and communicate things needs to be in focus.

In order for a "church" - a group of people who believe the truth about God and have become His children - to be planted in a community, there must first be church planters who are genuinely motivated by the love of Christ *for people*. Obviously they must be able to speak to people in a way that they understand, in their language, but along with that, there must also be people in the community who know and love these church planters, or at least respect them enough to have listened to what they have to say. This takes more than just knowing the right words to say in the right order. It takes relationships - where there is a degree of friendship and trust - because if there are no relationships, there will be no ministry.

A focus on people is something that the church planter must have practiced as he learned the language and culture while living his life as part of the community. Someone who is not engaged with people and has not developed relationships with people that draw them to the Lord will often find that when they try to share truth, people show a lack of interest, or 'hardness of heart' toward what they are wanting to share with them.

An essential element in communicating the Gospel is communicating God's love and care for people. God sent His own Son to save people, and so those communicating that message must actively show His love through their own lives, as His representatives. The Gospel is a personal, relational message of love from God to man and cannot be effectively communicated simply through theoretical facts in a formal way.

So, we said that church planting is a different undertaking essentially because it is God's work and anyone engaged in it is actually in partnership with Him. God is intimately involved and has been doing things already in the hearts of people to prepare them for the "arrival" of their opportunity to hear the Gospel. He has purposes that He wants to accomplish in their midst – these are the things that develop into the Church that *He* will plant there. A church planter should be conscious enough to notice these things, even from the very beginning when they are learning language and culture, and not be too caught up in their own plans to see His purposes. Many of the relationships that begin during culture and language learning may become important later on as a church develops.

What kind of program?

The best time to begin to live a life of interest and involvement in people's lives is when you first move into a community - which also happens to be when you start learning culture and language! This is the time when people will be most curious about you, and when you are the most vulnerable and will need the most help and support from them. It is a never-to-be-repeated time of opportunity to lean on people in the community to help you settle in, to help you find your feet and begin to learn about them, and for them to get to know you and begin to trust you.

So, for the long term goal of church planting, a language and culture learning program that requires a lot of community involvement and development of relationships is of great benefit to the final goal. A culture/language learning program like this would have the following overall features:

- A central focus on relationships with people as part of the learning process.

- The arena of language and culture learning activity is the life of the people.

- The means of reaching your goal of fluent communication is through activities that require relationships, first-hand experience with people, focusing on comprehension and communicative activities.

- A program that results in functional fluency - so you can speak in a natural way with people and have an intuitive understanding of how they are thinking and feeling as you speak.

What kind of learner?

The type of program is very important as it guides the activities and type of interaction that the learner might have in the community during the process of learning language and culture. But, perhaps an even more important, or foundational, aspect of the process of learning to communicate in a cross-cultural situation is the *attitude* of the person who is learning. Here are some notes made by a team leader who has worked for many years with cross-cultural church planters. He pinpoints some of the things he sees as being crucial for people as they go through the initial process of culture and language acquisition.

Some of the 'heart attitudes' necessary for a cross-cultural learner:

- *A high regard for culture* – this time is seen as an opportunity to comprehend the wide diversity in human existence and to find new opportunities for relationships.
- *An eagerness to learn* - welcoming the challenge in hopes of learning new facts, gaining new understandings, changing old opinions, shaping new interpretations, and making new commitments.
- *A desire to make connections* - being willing to persevere and use skills to build bridges and find common cultural ground, making an effort to form connections.
- *A readiness to give as well as receive* - not thinking in terms of personal gain, but in terms of opportunities for sharing.

We highly value language and culture learners who are:

- Curious (asking questions, rather than just passive)
- Trusting (rather than reacting with suspicion)
- Brave (rather than fearful, willing to take planned risks)
- Secure (confident in new situations, not afraid of failure)
- Relaxed (willing to adapt rather than being impatient)
- Teachable (ready for new experiences, to change and grow)
- Friendly (giving the first place to people, genuinely warm)
- Communicative (verbally and non-verbally - listening, observing, responding)
- Humble (and genuine)

- Compassionate and empathetic
- Motivated (for the correct reasons)

One last point that is a key to success in cross-cultural learning is the ability to both *accept* and *learn* from failure. When a person is in that position he can relax, accept failure as a normal part of the process and try things he knows will be flawed, for the purpose of learning and improving. He or she will be tolerant of his or her own mistakes and willing to learn from them.

? DISCUSSION POINTS

1. When you read the comments in the tutorial from the team leader about what he believes are helpful attitudes in a new learner, how does that make you feel? Are there particular characteristics mentioned there that you think you might be naturally more gifted in, or find easier, than others?

2. Do you think everyone can learn another language? Why or why not?

➡ ACTIVITIES

1. Imagine that you have decided to learn one of the world's major languages. Look online and list all of the different courses you could possibly take to learn that language if you chose to do so. Choose one course and give three reasons why you might choose that one.

2. Read the following article, *Culture Acquisition through getting close to people*.

Culture Acquisition[1] through getting close to people

The ultimate goals you and I have for ministry and how we imagine those goals might be achieved will shape the way in which we approach our relationships with others during CLA.

Is our ultimate goal for relationships to be able to 'get along' with people, or is it to be tolerated by a majority of people so that one day they will allow us to teach? Would we go further and describe our goals as 'knowing the culture' and 'speaking the language'?

Even these goals seem to fall short of what we understand genuine and effective ministry to require of us. The complex nature of cp and discipleship, and the objectives identified for seeing a Group come to maturity, demand a much deeper level of personal engagement — it is in fact who we are that is the key aspect of relating to others if we are to be effective in what we set out to do.

Giving people access to "us"

When someone approaches us personally with something to say, we instinctively begin to read many subtle clues in their interaction — we don't simply listen to the words they are saying, but, very quickly, we begin the work of trying to interpret much more complex issues:

What type of a person is this?

What is their real agenda — what are they wanting me to understand and why?

While they are talking to us, we gather and evaluate the more obvious information such as what they look like and the words they are speaking. At the same time we try to interpret what we know of their cultural and social background, aiming to answer the deeper questions we have about them. Understandably, and perhaps very sensibly, we want to know who they are before we are open to listen to or accept what they are trying to say.

In the same way, the people we desire to speak to will have questions about what type of person we are; they will want to answer those questions before they will truly hear the message we want to share. Inevitably, the cross-cultural problem we must face is that people will 'read' us — try to interpret who we are — based on their own view of the world, and according to the subtle signs that have specific meanings in their culture. If we never come to understand the meaning that these subtle cues convey, and consequently how people are really interpreting us, then we can't expect them to read us clearly or get to know who we are, or Who we represent. If they don't know us, they will

---

1. The assumption throughout this article is that culture and language are inseparable, and that culture acquisition and interaction requires language, but the major focus here is on aspects of culture acquisition.

struggle to 'hear' our message clearly.

For example, in many cultures, showing respect for other people's opinions is extremely important. Such respect is often shown in formal settings by patiently waiting for the appropriate time to speak and listening quietly to what others have to say before giving a personal opinion, which should then be given gently, and communicated as a suggestion rather than forcibly. It is tacitly understood that some people's opinions do have more value than others. But especially in a public forum, it is important that everyone be shown respect by being given an opportunity to be heard.

The weighing up of opinion and consequent decision-making is done in a subtle and lengthy way in order to maintain the appropriate level of respect. Jumping in and 'having our say' in such a setting in the same way we would in our own culture (Australian) would effectively communicate several things:

- we are not interested in anyone else's opinion
- we are rude and confrontational
- we are probably not people with whom it is going to be easy to work.

It might also cause the conversation to shut down entirely, or drive other people's voices and opinions on a certain topic 'underground'.

The only way to become skilled in all areas of communication is to spend time with people. By listening, observing and engaging in real life communication situations and actively practicing, improving our skills, evaluating and overcoming habits that hinder people's understanding of what we are trying to say, we will eventually become clear communicators within their cultural context. We must approach people with genuine humility and be willing to take the primary responsibility for clear communication. We need to 'bend over backwards' to get closer to people so they can clearly understand us and, eventually, our message.

It is equally important for those who will listen to have the opportunity to get to know us well and to learn to understand and trust us on their own terms. An Irish proverb says, "You must live with a person to know a person. If you want to know me, come and live with me."[2] CLA gives us the privilege of not only living among people to get to know them, but also gives them direct access to us, which helps them clearly see us and know who we are. Of course, Who we really want them to see is not us, but the Son in us. We should expect this process to be difficult, challenging and uncomfortable at times, but also very much 'worth it':

---

2. There are many cultural proverbs that express this same idea: "To understand the people you must first reach your neighbor" — a Chinese Proverb; "People learn from each other, but the most they learn from neighbors." — a Bulgarian Proverb.

Cross cultural ministry is like picking one's way through a mine field. With great care we probe for the mines, knowing that a situation may blow up in our face if we are careless. So we need to watch where the nationals walk, even where the pets walk, so reading cultural clues and cues. How are people reacting? Why are they reacting like they are? But hopefully we learn from errors and improve. To adapt to a people requires unusual flexibility and humility. Such ministry demands competent, intelligent and gifted servants of [the Father] ...[3]

As we continue to face the challenges of contextual communication, we have our Teacher's wonderful example; He gives the correct perspective and true meaning to the way we live among others. As we look to His example of becoming an insider, we will be thankful that we are pilgrims on the earth, enamored with the Son and sharing His purpose to serve people. He lived with clarity in regard to the culture He was within, challenging people to be reconciled to His Father in an appropriate (clearly communicated) way for them in their lives and cultural setting. The question is: How far are we prepared to go in following His example? Quite a challenging question, as Phil. 2:5 says, "You must have the same attitude that [He] had ..."

Being thoughtful and prepared

When I interact with another person, in my own culture or another, I should make it a habit to prepare myself and to think through the issues involved. As C.S. Lewis reflected, every single person we come into contact with is either on their way to eternity with God or on their way to an eternity without Him, and we have a responsibility to each one, either as a fellow believer or as someone who needs to know Him.

In order to be prepared to meet that responsibility, I could ask myself a few simple questions: What am I expecting? What are my goals in this relationship? What are my responsibilities? Do I want to communicate my message or allow God to communicate His message through me?

A few simple reminders could be helpful too: I am here to allow Him to meet their true needs through me (not to have my needs met). This isn't about me — it's about them. This relationship could be uncomfortable or costly for me — why am I willing to go through that discomfort or to pay that cost? I need the Lord's wisdom and strength to respond in the right way, and not how I often feel like responding!

CLA is pre-telling His story

The intention is not to compare my culture to another person's culture, but rather to recognize and do everything I can to minimize cultural hindrances so that the Father's message is as clear as possible for the people in their cultural context — I have to become an insider, able to communicate clearly in their context.

---

3. 'Introduction to Cross Cultural Ministry' by Jim Sutherland, Director, Reconciliation Ministries Network 1/2/1998 VI. Principles of Cross Cultural Ministry.

Before the people have access to His written Word or to hearing it taught, the pre-telling His story message is delivered through me. For better or worse, I am the communicator of His character — although they cannot yet see Him clearly, they can hopefully see some evidence of Him in the way I live.

We want the people to be intrigued and perhaps prompted to question certain assumptions they might have; *'Why would a person react in that way to such an embarrassing failure?'*; *'Why would someone still show kindness to someone who has wronged them?'*; *'What is motivating this person to live with discomfort like this?'*; *'Why do they care for me without expecting anything in return?'* Such questions are prompted by anomalies the people can see in our behavior that must point to underlying differences in our values and beliefs. If we behave in certain circumstances in a way different from what they would normally expect, then they may begin to ask *"Why?"*

Our goal is to become "insiders", but being an insider doesn't mean that we have to become exactly like people within that culture — our goal isn't to share all of their beliefs, values and behaviors. However, we do want to become insiders in the area of clear communication — we want them to know us and to be able to read us clearly because we have become skilled in communicating effectively within their parameters for communication. We want them to see that our values and beliefs are different, and to begin to question what might be the basis for that difference. Eventually, they will understand from His Word why we are different, and will personally be introduced to the One behind the differences. This kind of interaction with people has to be based on a foundation of putting other people's (ultimate, eternal) need above our own immediate needs.

Not perfect — just perfectly real

During CLA, or anytime, we shouldn't expect to live perfect lives before people; that's impossible — we are going to fail; we will have 'bad days', because we are human after all. This is especially true as we enter another cultural context where we are not aware of the specific things that could offend others or miscommunicate.

It can feel like a huge pressure for those of us trying to be His representatives and messengers among people if we think we have to be perfect and never make a mistake. The very fact that we are not perfect allows the Father to use us to show the people how a real, imperfect person lives before Him — the good news message lives in our lives in the way we model the day to day reality of the abundant life — and it will be Him who is shines through, not us.

When we do fail, how do we respond? Can we communicate through embarrassing or difficult circumstances that we care for people, are interested in them and are willing to persevere in seeking a relationship with them? We must be real — transparent and honest — before people so they will see that our reaction to failure or our own human weakness is based on something they don't yet understand. They will then feel free to be real with us and, more importantly, to be honest about themselves as they are introduced to the Father's character and realize their need for reconciliation to Him.

Empathy

Focusing on ourselves is common to man, a natural human response that we have to actively and continually practice denying in our relationships with others, until it becomes a habit of life. True empathy with others requires a disciplined turning away from self-focus and is an important foundational attitude necessary during CLA.

> *Empathy is related to, but distinct from, sympathy. If you have sympathy, you express pity or sorrow for the distress of another person. The sympathy, however, is determined by how you would feel if you were in that person's place. It is oriented to one's self. Since, you might say, I typically feel this way about such things, my friend probably feels this way too.*
>
> *If you have empathy, on the other hand, you can identify with the feelings of the other person on that person's terms. 'Empathy relies on the ability to temporarily set aside one's own perception of the world and assume an alternative perspective.' An empathetic person picks up seemingly disconnected cues and makes coherent sense out of them ... I recall the empathetic participants in our programs overseas — those who were less concerned about their own first-day nervousness than about the insecurities of the host Group as its members welcomed a stranger into their homes. On field trips they were the ones to empathize with the tour guide whose voice quivered because she had never explained the factory before to a group of visitors.*[4]

One of the key elements in being a truly empathetic person is focusing on the other person and deciding not to focus on myself. In a broader sense the CLA program with its Tenets and Principles was developed out of a basic desire to encourage an outward focus — on what the Father is doing — from the beginning of the process of Culture / Language Acquisition. Our tendency seems to be to focus on our learning, or our goals, rather than on the true needs of the people we live among; an inward focus in CLA is unhelpful in the short-term but can also carry into self-focused rather than Group-focused ministry.

So the principle behind culture-driven and relationship-centered CLA is the desire to see the cultivation of habits in learning and life that will nourish truly empathetic and people-focused servants of the Group. We (the Body in our time) have been greatly affected by the thinking that it is what happens *internally* that is important, and that the most important work the Father is doing is *in me*. In a broader cultural sense, the messages we constantly hear from the world lead us to think that each individual person is

---

4. J. Daniel Hess, The Whole World Guide to Culture Learning (1994) p19.

the center of his own universe: *"It's all about YOU." "Go ahead — you know you deserve it."*

This cultural thread has been there (from the garden of Eden), but has increased hugely in recent days until selfishness is a major theme of the global culture. As we enter CLA we must clearly evaluate how selfishness has affected our own thinking. It is good to remind ourselves often that we are not the most important element in the whole scheme of things; we need to take our eyes off ourselves and focus on more interesting things, such as what He is doing. We are privileged to serve with Him — His co-workers in what He is doing right now through His Body. So, the Tenets and Principles of CLA are not only a 'good idea' or a 'good way for us to learn culture and language', they are also an attempt to shape the way we go about our learning and interaction with others by the realities of the way we see our Father working in the world.

Knowing individuals well will give us a more realistic view

When we think about our home country and people in our own neighborhood, we can no doubt see a significant level of cultural similarity between us and our neighbors as a group. However, when we think of individuals within that group, there are probably some significant variations in belief, values, opinions, life experience, goals, fears, and many other areas depending on who the individuals are. These things could affect how each person would accept or reject new ideas and also how we would relate to each person as an individual. A culture is in many aspects 'homogeneous' — having a uniform composition or structure — but it is not only that, it is also an extremely complex mix of personalities and opinions, experiences and values and is made up of a variety of individuals.

Cultural 'themes' are observations that can be made that generally apply to people within a culture — they describe the homogenous aspects of culture — generalizations about a certain cultural group. It is helpful to observe and attempt to describe these more general themes in culture, especially toward the end of CLA. However, description of themes should not be seen as the ultimate goal of culture acquisition. Do all of the cultural themes attributed to your own culture apply to you personally? For example, here are theme statements about Australian life:

> *Australians are very friendly and helpful people, with a great sense of humor and a natural ability to tell jokes and play with words. Sometimes Australians may appear cold because of our "private nature". Australians were born to compete — Australia is considered one of the most competitive nations on earth — this covers all areas of life including the work place. It is amazing how passionately Australians feel about fishing. Australians are compulsive buyers having some of the biggest credit card debts in the world. Australians are very informal when it comes to clothes.*[5]

These statements probably apply to many Australians and give a general view of common attitudes and lifestyles, but somebody meeting an Australian person for the first

---

5. Excerpts are from a website explaining the Australian lifestyle to visitors from Latin America.

time shouldn't assume that he loves fishing, has a large credit card debt and likes to joke around.

Cultural themes should only be applied to a culture as a whole, not attributed to every individual within that culture with whom we interact.

Development of overall cultural themes can only take place over a long period of time after getting to know a large number of individuals well. We cannot expect to adequately identify cultural themes by 'standing outside' of a culture. Going through a process of becoming part of that culture, through knowing people well, is essential. When we get close to people we will begin to understand the complexity of belief underlying their behaviors and values. We will then have a chance to develop an intuitive feel for the scope and depth of how overall cultural themes actually apply to individuals within the culture.

In our own interaction with the US culture, through many friends and visits to the USA, we quickly identified some important cultural themes — the Group, security, freedom, responsibility, etc. However, we also quickly made some assumptions and generalizations about US culture without really knowing enough of a variety of individuals within that culture, or to a deep enough level to do so. Our natural tendency is to draw conclusions too quickly, based on our own culture and worldview, which tends to skew our interaction with people because we have made presuppositions about their personal motivations and feelings. We can be too quick to develop ideas about themes and apply these to everyone before we have enough of a foundation to do so.

So, an important principle for CLA is that we must begin by getting to know individuals before making any general assumptions about their culture. This step cannot be missed out, it is essential. We want to get to the point of relationship with people where we understand the motivation for their behavior — what they value, what they believe in, what embarrasses them, what they fear, who they trust, what makes them feel comfortable and relaxed. In building a strong foundation of these kinds of pieces of the picture through getting to know individuals well, we can, over time, build a realistic and practical view of the whole community. We will know instinctively what are some generally held principles or opinions, but we will also understand that not everyone in the community will hold to those.

Some friends of ours in PNG, for example, live in a village community where the concept of 'privacy' is not something that most people value or even think about. We were surprised when our friends told us one day that they find it difficult in the village setting that everyone knows everyone else's business; they longed for a bit more privacy. We had assumed they didn't think about privacy at all.

A few years ago we were talking to a young guy in Mexico about the culture there. He was born in Tijuana then went to the States where he grew up and lived most of his life, but for the last seven years he has been back living and studying in Mexico. He told of a visit he and two friends made to town to meet with another friend. They waited in the agreed place in the city, but the agreed time of the meeting passed and their friend didn't show up. He related what happened next: "The time went by and I got angry, you know! So my friend said to me, 'Hey man, what's up?' So I said, 'He should be here now, he's late, where is he!?' And my friend, he said, 'Take it easy, relax, what are you angry about?' And then my friend kind of laughed and said, 'Welcome to your culture!'"

Avoiding assumptions

How do we approach an individual to relate with them? What are we thinking about that person? Is our uppermost thought, "This person is a Mexican, or an Indian, or a Papua New Guinean, therefore they are different to me in specific cultural ways." We often come with preconceived ideas, based on what we already know, or think we know, about their culture.

A good way to approach someone is to try to minimize the differences and to see them as a man or a woman just like myself — an interesting person with a life that I want to know about, probably with many of the same thoughts and feelings I have, certainly with similar emotional responses in many situations, and definitely a spiritual need that is common to all people. They will have many different life experiences, thoughts and opinions that I can learn from. I must recognize that our communication patterns are different, so I have to be sensitive to their communication rules and understand those in order to get to know the person underneath; and for them to really get to know me I need to be aware of the way I am communicating. Our perception of how we 'acquire culture' or gain an understanding of culture can have a definite effect on how we approach people — as individuals whom we would like to get to know, or as a piece of a cultural puzzle that we would like to figure out.

Why do we need to understand culture at this level? Isn't the Father the One to communicate Himself to the people we are living among? Yes, He longs to communicate with people and has chosen the best possible way to do that — through people. Through us! We are one of His primary methods of communication. Our very lives are speaking, not just when we open our mouths — we need to be insiders to the degree that we understand people and culture well enough to communicate clearly through how we live. As we get to know individuals well, we can predict how our behavior and our words will be "read" by them — we will know what meaning they attribute to our lives, and if we are giving a clear message or not. When we reach this level of understanding, we are then able to communicate the Father's message, person to person, getting through cultural layers to the person underneath — a human being standing before their Creator, just as we are.

Being messengers requires sacrifice

A complex culture made up of individuals needs an adequate response. The Father Himself has communicated through His Word, which is a whole body of truth. His message meets all the possible individual responses and individual hearts within a group of people hearing it; the message is more than adequate. We have the privilege and responsibility of being His means of communication by presenting His message through our lives and in delivering His Word effectively. A deep and intuitive understanding of culture will help us "stay out of His way" as He communicates to them through us. We become like them — in the way we communicate — in order that He can clearly communicate what He wants to say through us.

CLA is not a collection of language and culture learning techniques, or a way to 'study' a culture and analyze a language. The CLA program contains all of these things but it is essentially a lifestyle that involves a continuous commitment to become someone else — to get inside the thinking of individuals — to do the things that may be uncomfortable and difficult each day to grow into a clear conduit for the Father's communication. When we are truly engaged in CLA it takes our whole person, and a conscious connection to our Maker who supplies our need to live it and helps us to remain humble and flexible.

Living among and reaching out to people of another culture and language is not a natural or easy thing to do. Discomfort in stepping out of our own cultural context is a common human tendency. We see evidence of this struggle all over the world: ethnic minority groups living within a wider foreign culture while retaining, sometimes for generations, their own cultural identity, or sub-groups within culture whose members enjoy and celebrate the fact that they share some common interest, activity or lifestyle. It is more natural and more comfortable for people of the same cultural background to stick together — we enjoy security and understanding; most of us actively seek it out and avoid situations where these factors don't exist. For many of us our home culture and environment is for the most part a socially comfortable place. We have learned to function there, we have recognizable cultural cues, we are surrounded by loved and trusted people, or at least people whom we understand and who understand us — we fit in. Things are familiar and we can face the world, on most days, with confidence.

Launching into an unfamiliar cultural situation in order to learn and become a part of a community can be extremely difficult, extremely uncomfortable and extremely challenging! What a vulnerable place to be! But we have this treasure in earthen vessels that the power may be of Him and not of us; so we can confidently move into an unfamiliar and uncomfortable situation with humility and reliance upon His Spirit within us for wisdom. He wants us to be His communicators even though we are weak and vulnerable, so that He will shine through.

We can trust Him for the opportunities to meet and develop friendships with individuals within that community and for them to have access to us as individuals as well. We can even trust Him to use our failures to show Himself to people. We are able to engage with confidence in a new community setting simply by approaching individual people that He brings us into contact with, having these initial goals: "I want to talk to you. I am interested in knowing you and understanding your culture. I want to get to know you as a person and I want you to get to know me too."

Becoming part of a community and making friends, developing lifetime relationships, and possibly relationships that will last for eternity, is also a fascinating, wonderful and rewarding experience — it can be great fun and it is a huge privilege for us to be in that position.

We can learn much that is helpful for CLA from Paul as he describes his interaction with the Thessalonians and how his relationship with them developed:

For we speak as messengers approved by [the Father] to be entrusted with the Good News. Our purpose is to please [Him], not people. He alone examines the motives of our hearts. Never once did we try to win you with flattery, as you well know. And [He] is our witness that we were not pretending to be your friends just to get your money! As for human praise, we have never sought it from you or anyone else.

As apostles of [the Son] we certainly had a right to make some demands of you, but instead we were like children among you. Or we were like a mother feeding and caring for her own children. We loved you so much that we shared with you not only [His] Good News but our own lives, too.

Don't you remember, dear brothers and sisters, how hard we worked among you? Night and day we toiled to earn a living so that we would not be a burden to any of you as we preached [His] Good News to you. You yourselves are our witnesses — and so is [He] — that we were devout and honest and faultless toward all of you believers. And you know that we treated each of you as a father treats his own children. We pleaded with you, encouraged you, and urged you to live your lives in a way that [He] would consider worthy. For he called you to share in his Kingdom and glory. (1 Thess. 2:4-12 - NLT)

4.17 Culture/Language acquisition 2

OBJECTIVES OF THIS TUTORIAL

This tutorial continues to discuss the important principles of Culture/Language acquisition, in particular what level of fluency and understanding should we be aiming for? How well do we really need to communicate to have an effective role in a community? Looking into the complexity of the communication landscape in our own language and culture is the first step to understanding the fluency level required when learning another language and culture.

Introduction

"Some of the most remarkable events in this world pass unnoticed because they occur so frequently. It should by any standard be considered remarkable that human beings can communicate their inward thoughts to each other at all, other than by facial expression and gestures. After all, any given language uses a very restricted range of sounds, whereas the number of meanings that people communicate is infinite. Yet, with a range of between twenty and forty distinctive sounds available to them, people communicate this infinity of meaning effortlessly, constantly, and completely, heedless of the magnitude of their achievement."

- Kathleen Callow, Man and Message

Most of us talk to other people quite often every day - achieving this remarkable thing called human communication - probably without giving the actual process of communication a second thought. And we have been doing it since we were children. That picture changes dramatically when we find ourselves in a cross-cultural situation and begin to try to communicate in another language and cultural context - even simple things like trying to find a bathroom suddenly become an adventure in misunderstanding, and it is clear that communication isn't such a natural or easy thing at all!

In this tutorial we want to focus on some of the complexities that exist in communication in your *own* language and cultural situation, and to look at some of the "nuts and bolts" of what is actually going on when people are talking. Understanding the great number of interrelated things that are going on in order for clear communication to take place in your own language will open the way to seeing what it might take to become an effective communicator in another language and culture.

Components of interpersonal communication

We are going to look more closely at some of the things that are going on when people communicate with one another; when they have conversations, give instructions, teach, speak or in any way converse. Your goal isn't to try to memorize all of these things, but simply to try to broaden your view and think about the whole *landscape* in which communication takes place and how effective communication is a bigger picture than just putting words into sentences. You will notice that it is more than just the *words* a person is saying that actually communicate to another person, but communication is affected by many other things, such as the context of the conversation, the relationship the speakers have, the information they share and how they go about organizing what they say in particular ways to achieve their purpose.

As you work through this tutorial, take the opportunity to observe in an informal way, some of the underlying things that are happening in real conversations around you in order for the miracle of communication to take place.

The context

The first thing to notice about a conversation is the context in which it is taking place - the background or 'landscape' in which it is happening:

- Where is it taking place? (The physical location and cultural setting, the time, any other significant situational cues - what the occasion is…)
- Who are the speakers? (Gender, age, dress, status…)
- What do you know about the relationships between the participants? (Family members, strangers…)
- What tone of voice is being used? (Normal conversational level, yelling, whispering, authoritative, gentle…)
- What is the major issue being addressed?
- What are the social circumstances surrounding the conversation or speech? (The social scene in which it took place. Were there other listeners, did anyone interject, were the speakers trying to keep their conversation private in any way?)
- What reasons, values and beliefs are referred to, or implied?
- What overt indicators are there of any emotional reaction to the things that are said, by the participants or listeners? (facial expressions, non-verbal communication…)

- Are any of the participants members of a subculture or social group within the community?
- What role or position does each person seem to be taking in the conversation? (Commanding, persuasive, passive, receptive, submissive, resistant...)

The background 'landscape' of a conversation is the first thing to notice, but there are also other important elements that will help you to understand the communication that is taking place.

The level of shared understanding

Everything we say is effected by who we're saying it to, how much shared information and shared experiences we have. The way I communicate - how much, how fast, what style, what tone, mostly how much I leave out and put in - is all determined by the relationship and understanding that I share with the person I'm talking to.

When people communicate, they may already share a vast amount of information that forms a foundation for their conversation, things that they already know and therefore don't need to articulate. This shared information could include the details of the surroundings, relevant events both recent and more distant, shared plans and purposes, shared social or family relationships, weather patterns, common household objects and utensils, common behavior patterns, specialized knowledge, experiences and attitudes related to that place - these and countless other factors in daily life are shared by people in a community. When you observe a particular conversation, try to identify whatever you can about the shared information or areas of common interest that exist between the participants. In other words, what is the shared base for conversation? The following questions will help you.

- How is 'common ground' sought and found and how is it shared?
- What evidence is there of shared information? (events, people, relationships, knowledge, experience?)
- Does the speaker include oblique references to other conversations or situations?
- Is any of the language used esoteric (difficult to understand by outsiders, or secretive and confidential), or is it language accessible to all members of the community? If esoteric terms are used, are they explained?
- Think about the participants' mutual awareness - each knows, for the given situation, who may speak and who may not, what topics are relevant, what degree of formality or casualness is required, how long the conversation may reasonably continue. Note any clues in this communication situation that point to the level of mutual awareness and how the participants feel about one another. (Love or resentment, trust or have reservations, like or dislike, sense of humor, sense of self...)

- Identify possible indicators in the way the speakers are communicating that they might be adjusting to the closeness or distance from the other person. For example: the form of speech, the content, style, register, amount of detail, asserting, envisaging, imagining, the way they refers to people, how the message develops, the pace of information, the examples or illustrations used, themes, the viewpoint expressed and with how much certainty, the evaluations made, attitudes, tone of voice, type of language - all may be indicators of adjustment to the person or people being spoken to.

The purpose

Our purpose in communicating shapes everything we say. When we listen to someone we always unconsciously ask: What kind of talk is this? Is the speaker telling? Explaining? Ordering? What does he want us to do? If the hearer can't answer those questions - he can't process the communication - a listener is always unconsciously trying to 'work out' the underlying purpose of the speaker.

- What seems to have prompted the talk or conversation? Is it to exchange information (informational)? Is it to effect change (volitional)? Is it to share emotions and attitudes (expressive)?
- What might be the speaker's purpose in communicating? What does he want the audience or other participant to hear and understand?
- Does the speaker state his purpose clearly? Is it clear only by implication?
- What does the speaker expect listeners or other participants to do after listening to him?
- Is it clear from his talk what the speaker's position is? Where and how does the speaker's position become clear?
- In what specific ways does the speaker indicate his purpose?
- What relationship do you think the speaker might be seeking to establish with his hearers?
- What does the speaker seem to presume listeners wish to know more about?
- How does the speaker attempt to achieve his purpose in communication? Was he successful? Why or why not?
- Does the hearer indicate that he is monitoring or trying to understand the speaker's purpose? (If it's not clear, we may say so: "I'm not sure what you're driving at", "So where is this taking us?", "Why do you ask that?". Uncertainty about purpose makes for awkwardness, hesitancy, etc. Conversation can flow naturally and freely only in the context of some area of shared purpose.) Look for any indications of the hearer searching for the speaker's purpose.

The hearer

When we communicate, we monitor the hearer's knowledge, comprehension, reactions, and social status. We adjust the shape of the message: slow it down, speed it up, fill in background information, put in signposts - because we know that if the hearer doesn't understand the message, he/she can't retain the message.

- Think about the effect of the speaker's talk on the listener. Can they follow him easily (comprehension)? Are they reacting to what he is saying (acceptance)?
- Was he misunderstood, and if so, what specifically did he do about it? (Repeat himself, slow down his speech, restate it in a different way, use illustrations, examples or questions to further explain any point...)
- How did the misunderstanding seem to affect the participants emotionally? (Did they seem embarrassed, irritable, defensive?)
- Did his speech initiate a reaction of any kind and if so, what did he do about it?
- Notice how questions are asked, how incorrect answers are dealt with and how questions are answered.
- How do the relationships between those involved in the conversation affect the way the speaker adjusts the shape of his message?
- How direct is the mode of address and what do you think this indicates?

The main idea

A key characteristic of communication is that we store life's experiences in our minds in organized ways and the way we express what we want to communicate is also organized in similar fashion. One of the keys to whether or not our message gets across will be whether or not people share the same frames of reference needed to process the information and whether we've said enough to make those frames of reference clear to our hearers.

The reason we organize what we say is that not everything is equally important. There are some things that are more important and some things that are just meant to stay in the background. The important things need to be clearly understood and should clearly be the *theme* of what is being said. Every language has ways of indicating what is important and what isn't, because if people don't know what the theme is, they won't understand what we are talking about! In other words - the message will be blurred, like a sign that sends the wrong message - and people will be trying to sort out the details from the main point.

So, notice how the *theme* is indicated in conversations in your own language by thinking about the following:

- What is the general topic or main idea of the talk or conversation?

- What is the general subject area that it covers?
- What other main ideas are covered?
- Does it seem to be an important conversation? Why or why not?
- How does the speaker indicate his major theme or point and when it is clearly introduced or indicated?
- Has the speaker organized his communication? (Can it be broken into sub-sections?)
- How does the speaker introduce and develop his or her ideas? Does the speaker compare or contrast? Use anecdotes? Develop by example? Tell a story? Appeal to authority (other sources) or to his or her own character/expertise? Describe a process? Evaluate? Notice how these things are organized in the talk or conversation.
- Think about the possible reasons the speech is organized and developed the way it is. What does the speaker do first, second, third, etc. Why?
- Does the organization seem primarily driven by content, the speaker's argument, or audience expectations?
- What does the speaker emphasize or spend the most time on? Why do you think that is?
- What is considered background information? Identify specific pieces of background information that are mentioned.

Dividing the information

When we communicate, we have ways of processing large amounts of information by dividing it into manageable pieces, so that there is a much greater probability that we will be understood, and our listeners won't get 'lost'. Every language has ways of dividing information into separate pieces. When there's a change in participants, events, time or location there's usually a well-defined indicator or sign that we are moving on to a new piece of information.

- Identify any changes in theme in the conversation. List all of the changes that you notice - participants, events, time, location.
- What signs or codes are used and understood to indicate where a new piece of information is introduced? Identify as much as possible the different ways that a new piece of information is introduced. (Specific words or non-verbal cues?)
- Notice how the various pieces of information are introduced, ordered and presented. What are the relationships between the themes and the order they are introduced and what significance do you think that has?

Tying thoughts together

As well as dividing information into pieces, we also make sure that we tie our thoughts together. People presume that what they are hearing is going to make sense and fit together - they're listening for that as they go along so they know how to process the information and store it. Lack of cohesion is one of the biggest reasons people can't follow what we've said and share it with someone else…

- How does the speaker link the various parts of what he is saying together to make the whole understandable to his audience? He may use particular words at the beginning or end of paragraphs, he may indicate old or new information, or repeat the names of specific people, places, times or actions to make sure people know 'where they are' and what is going on.

- How does the sequence of ideas flow and how are the various ideas spaced out or separated? What is it that holds them together or relates one thought to another?

- Do the ties used to hold thoughts together influence the meaning one way or another?

- What patterns do you notice in the 'ties' that the speaker uses to hold thoughts together in this example of communication?

Keeping track of the actors

Languages have lots of different ways of 'labeling' the various actors on stage, and English is no exception. It has many forms to refer to the same person - *he, that guy, Steve, the accountant, Mary's father, our mutual friend, Stevo*, etc. - and there are good reasons why and when we would use each one. In another language, careful study is needed so we know why the different forms are used and when, it isn't just a case of learning the words for 'he' and 'she'. For now, notice in conversations in your own language how we keep track of who is doing what. Everyone wants to know who's doing what - it's an important part of the message.

- Who are the participants mentioned by the speaker?

- Are all the participants referred to in the same way? List the participants and the various ways the speaker refers to each one. (Openly by name, obliquely, pronouns, nicknames, implication)

- Think about why the speaker refers to different participants in different ways, or the same participant in a variety of ways? What does it indicate both in terms of the understandability of the message and the feeling of the speaker toward the participants?

- Are there misunderstandings regarding participants and how does the speaker clarify these?

CULTURE/LANGUAGE ACQUISITION 2

Keeping track of who said what

We very seldom just talk about people *doing* things, a lot of what we say is about people *saying* things. All languages have complicated ways of signaling who is saying what to whom. Notice how this is indicated.

- How does the speaker signal that some other person said something? Notice how the speaker introduces the quote, how he gives the quote, and then how he indicates that it is finished.
- Are all quotes introduced in the same way? Gather many different forms of quotes from different speakers and in different situations so you understand the variety of forms of communicating who said what.
- Are there misunderstandings regarding 'who said what' and if so, how does the speaker clarify these?

Keeping it interesting

We want people to stay engaged with what we are saying, so we try very hard to make it interesting. In English, we don't just use metaphors and illustrations - we have lots of ways to stretch words and 'not say what we mean' (look up definitions of each of these):

- Euphemisms
- Litotes
- Hyperbole
- Sarcasm
- Irony
- Metonymy
- Synecdoche
- Personification
- Apostrophe
- Idioms

Almost everything we say is figurative. Very little that we say does not 'skew' - make the form different from the meaning - to make what we say more interesting to our hearers. We have a *million* ways to show feeling, emotion, emphasis, highlighting, evaluations...

- What are the various ways used by the speaker/s to make their talk more interesting?
- Try to identify the speaker's specific purpose in using figurative language at that

point. What was he trying to communicate, to highlight, or to emphasize?

- Notice if and how the audience or other participants react to the figurative language used.
- Do some people use more figurative language than others, how does that reflect on their personalities or role or status in the community?

Observing interpersonal communication

This week, try to actively observe the conversations happening around you, or that you are taking part in. Take notice of:

The communication 'landscape':

- the context,
- the level of shared understanding
- the purpose
- the main idea

The things speakers do to communicate their message -

- dividing the information
- tying thoughts together
- keeping track of the actors
- keeping track of who said what
- keeping it interesting

As you observe people communicating with one another and think about all that is involved, remember that all of these things happen in other languages too, but they happen in *different ways*. One of the major mistakes people make when they learn and try to communicate in another language is that they bring over the forms of interpersonal communication from their own language and culture - they may learn the *words* of the new language but never really learn to *communicate* in the way that local people do. The purpose of us investigating underlying communication patterns in our own language is so that we understand that we will also need to observe and learn these 'big picture' aspects in another language, in order to communicate a clear message.

CULTURE/LANGUAGE ACQUISITION 2

? DISCUSSION POINTS

1. Have you noticed different forms or patterns of communication that non-native speakers of English bring over to their English communication from their original language? Do you notice the same non-English patterns appearing in different people from the same language background? Why would that be the case?

2. Do you have any observations about your own style of communication and how you usually try to get your message across? Are there things you have never thought about before or anything you would like to change to improve your effectiveness as a communicator?

➡ ACTIVITIES

1. Record a short video conversation between two or three people (from TV, online, or an actual event). Watch the video as many times as you need to make notes on each of the components of interpersonal communication mentioned in the tutorial.

2. Read the article, *What does 'Fluency' really mean?* (next page). It was written by a language and culture consultant to paint a picture of the end goal of cross-cultural workers for their language learning time, before they were considered fluent enough to enter into "ministry".

What does "Fluency" really mean?

An understanding of what is meant by "Fluency" is essential if one is to attain that goal in functional ability in another language and culture. In the following article this will be discussed from a practical point of view.

Proficiency in another language and culture really has little to do with test scores and more to do with how a person can actually function in life situations. In light of this you might ask yourself a couple of questions: "What would I like to do when I move to a new country, where people live differently than I do and speak another language than mine? How would I like to be able to eventually function in that new setting?"

In thinking about the goals for your interaction in the host culture, there are several things to consider. As a believer you have a clear purpose for being in the country and a special message to communicate with others. Yet in order to achieve these purposes, you will first need to integrate as well as possible and not always seem like the out-of-place foreigner. While you will always be someone from another place and culture, your goal is to become someone who understands and acts in appropriate ways in spite of your place and language of origin — not always drawing attention to yourself, consciously or unconsciously.

Getting to a point of interacting this way in the host culture does not happen all at once. Becoming "normal" to others around you in that new setting is a gradual process. And you do want to be a normal citizen in the community, even though you come from another country. So what does this goal of "normal" look like for you? What areas should you think about as you grow more comfortable in this way?

One important area to consider in becoming a normal or ordinary member of society has to do with the fact that ordinary citizens can communicate about everyday life events. They can discuss current events with their neighbors or acquaintances and even strangers. Eventually you will want to be able to do this as well in order to fit in with them. True, even after you can manage this process quite well, sometimes these events will be beyond your understanding since the community members around you will enter into cultural domains you are not familiar with. This may even stretch your vocabulary, giving you opportunities to learn more vocabulary and culture. You may find your language deteriorating somewhat in this new situation. But when you have gained the appropriate ability and find yourself in this kind of situation, you are able to recognise that this area is new to you. So you simply cope by asking the appropriate questions to learn and participate as much as possible in the conversation in spite of your limitations.

Another important area of learning is that ordinary citizens can also build deep friendships because they have the cultural understanding and language ability to do so. They know how intently they want to pursue those friendships and how to do that effectively if the other person shows the same interest. This involves knowing and understanding the life and cultural context of that person in a real, experiential way. Such relationships need to include the ability to talk about life issues that affect that person and the circumstances that they are going through. So as you grow in your understanding and ability to communicate in your new context, you also need to learn to do this.

The fact is that in spite of your efforts to fit in, living in a foreign culture like this presents many instances where you can unintentionally offend others. As you adjust to your new culture, you will learn to recognise when this has happened, or you will know who might be able to help you figure out what has happened and what you should do. In this way you can learn to follow the appropriate actions for reconciliation. Even so, there still may be times when you are unaware of what you have done that caused offence or even of the fact that you have caused offence.

As is the case in all societies, different members of society will hold differing views and opinions. They will have reasons for this, of course, and will express those reasons, even defend them. You, likewise, will desire the ability to give your opinions appropriately and explain the reasons why you hold those beliefs. This would be considered important, "normal" interaction that must take place between friends and acquaintances.

As a believer, you also have the desire to speak into the lives of your friends and influence them for good. You will want them to have the same knowledge about God that you have. In obedience to the commission given to you as His servant, you will seek to make disciples. Through the process of becoming an ordinary citizen you will have gained the ability to teach God's Word to those who are interested or to give a testimony of your faith to even a stranger, when the opportunity is there to do so.

As a believer you also have the desire to be part of a local church. As a functioning member of the church in that context, you will want to have the ability to comprehend the teaching of Scripture and also to make comment when Scripture is discussed. All of God's children have been gifted for the benefit of the church, and gaining normal ability will allow you to use your gifts in the context of a local body, even one in your host culture.

Another area that would demonstrate normal ability is the ability to talk about your plans and what might happen if unforeseen circumstances arise. This might still be difficult for you, but you should be able to do so in certain domains, especially ones you have become very familiar with.

Even though you can do all of these things, you are far, very far, from being "native-like" in your speech and interactions. You may even have some pronunciation issues to keep dealing with. Your speech will be far from perfect or even grammatically correct at all times. Although you won't have consistent patterns of error in your speaking, you will still confuse grammatical features in the language from time to time. This will particularly be the case when you get into domains you are not familiar with. Your use of subtleties in discourse, body language, tone of voice, and other non-linguistic cues might be lacking to a great degree at times. But in your overall interactions, these "gaps" will not have a great affect on your ability to be a part of normal life, nor will they confuse your listeners to any significant degree.

So how does this sound? Does this sound like what you would like to be able to do? Would you like to be on a path of continual growth and learning in your host culture? If so, you desire what we label "fluency". What is even more important is your desire to be a functioning member of your host community in a wide variety of areas.

4.18 Becoming a communicator 1

OBJECTIVES OF THIS TUTORIAL

This tutorial discusses some key skills needed for culture and language acquisition - listening and observation.

Introduction

Two of the most important skills needed for language and culture acquisition are listening and observation. The most successful learners spend a lot of time early on just *listening and observing* - listening to the sounds, tones, and stresses of the language and also when and how people are speaking, and carefully observing what is going on around them. Both of these skills may seem like passive activities, but in fact they require thought and discipline and even take some practice to become good at. Most people are not naturally great listeners or observers, so we will be looking at some ways to practice these skills even while you are still in your own cultural setting.

Active Listening

"Hearing is passive, listening is active. Understanding the difference between hearing and listening is an important prerequisite for listening effectively."

Dr. John Kline

In the Yanomamo tribal language, *jiliyao* means to hear, and *jiliblao*, to listen actively. This recognises the fact that hearing and listening are actually two different activities.

In the last tutorial we talked about the *communication landscape* - and identified the components of interpersonal communication - we saw that there are many more contributing factors to clear communication than only the words that are being spoken. So it follows that when we listen in order to learn how to communicate, we probably shouldn't just listen to the words; *"To study language by listening only to utterances, is to miss as much as 75 percent of the meaning"* David McNeil.

It has been said that communication is:
- 7% verbal - words
- 38% vocal - volume, pitch, rhythm, tone, stress
- 55% body movements - mostly facial expressions

Barriers to good listening

The fact is that we typically retain, for a few minutes, only 65% of what is said to us - and two months later, our recall is down to 25% of what we were told. Why is this? Below are some of the common barriers to good listening. Most of us will recognise at least some of these 'bad habits' - either because we have had them done to us or we may even do them ourselves...

- Constantly *comparing* yourself to the speaker (Who is smarter? Who's had it rougher? This is too hard for me.)
- Trying to *mind read* what the speaker really thinks (He probably thinks I'm stupid for saying that.)
- *Planning* what argument or story to give next.
- *Filtering* so that you hear only certain topics or don't hear critical remarks.
- *Judging* a statement to be "crazy," "boring," "hostile," etc. before it is completed.
- *Daydreaming*.
- *Remembering* your own personal experiences instead of listening to the speaker.
- Busily drafting your prescription or *advice* long before the speaker has finished.
- Considering every conversation an intellectual *debate* with the goal of putting down the opponent.
- Believing you are *always right* so don't need to listen.
- Quickly *changing the topic* or laughing it off if the topic gets serious.
- *Placating* the other person ("You're right...Of course...I agree...Really!") by automatically agreeing with everything.

Qualities of a good listener

So, what are the qualities of a *good* listener? Typically we all practice good listening some of the time, especially if we are interested in a topic or genuinely want to get to know someone better. These are attitudes and skills we need to become aware of, to begin to practice and to seek to do more automatically - because to become a good communicator, one of the first steps is to practice active listening as a skill, attitude and eventually a habit of life.

Characteristics of a good listener:

- Pays attention.
- Is attentive and active, not focused on formulating responses.
- Listens with objectivity, to discover what the speaker thinks (doesn't transfer preconceived personal beliefs to the speaker).
- Does not judge the speaker before hearing him out.
- Verifies understanding, and only responds after understanding.
- Restates key points to affirm understanding and build further dialogue.
- Summarizes key points to affirm understanding and build further dialogue.
- Asks (non-threatening) questions to build understanding.

Observation

"To acquire knowledge, one must study; but to acquire wisdom, one must observe."

- Marilyn vos Savant

Observation is something we do all the time as a natural course of life, but if someone intends to learn how to relate naturally in another culture, observation needs to be a skill that is honed and developed. Often there are insights into culture that we can miss if we don't actively observe patterns of behavior and try to fit those into a framework to understand why people are doing the things we see them doing.

Observation is one of the primary methods of gathering information for someone in the early stages of cross-cultural learning. It is particularly valuable because it helps someone to view actual behavior - rather than socially pressured or conditioned statements. For example, think about what you might answer if someone asked you, "What time do you get up in the morning?" You would probably give a single time that is an ideal (when you would like to get up, or think you should get up) or an average of the time you usually get up. Now, think about the picture someone would get if they were able to *observe* your morning routine for two weeks - would the answer that you gave initially be true all of the time or most of the time? Do you get up the same time on weekends as weekdays? Observing behavior rather than just asking a question is the difference between the *ideal* and the *real* - what people say and what they actually do can sometimes be different, and you can get a better picture if you are a careful observer.

People who are astute observers often end up being more "natural" participants in the culture, because they have learned how local people behave, have seen the gestures they use, noted the facial expressions and tone of voice that is used in different circumstances. Naturalness is important to clear communication, because it allows people to listen without being distracted by the confusing messages given by 'unusual' behavior.

Of course, later on when a person can speak and understand the language more fluently they will be able to investigate more deeply the motivation for certain behavior and gain more of an insight into a person's thinking, by talking to them - but observation will always be an important part of understanding what is going on.

Good observation is simply noticing the *details*:

- The physical location:
    - What is the setting? (where the situation is taking place, what kind of a room or building or setting, what people are wearing, what props or objects are involved - anything of note)
    - What kind of a situation is it? (formal or informal, people's purpose for being there, etc.)
- The human interactions:
    - How many people are involved?
    - Who are they? (gender, ages, social group, etc.)
    - How are they related? (strangers, workmates, relatives, business relationship)
- Communication:
    - What kind of communication is taking place? (verbal, non-verbal, formal or informal, etc.)
    - Who is communicating to whom and how?
- Timelines:
    - What is the sequence of events?
    - Was something going on before you arrived?
- Questions:
    - Write down any questions you have that come to mind for future reference (anything you would like to investigate or understand more about, people in the situation you might talk to later, things you can find out later)

Practice is necessary to become a good observer, but there is a lot of opportunity to practice! It is a good thing to seek to develop a healthy curiosity about what is going on around you and to notice the details in a situation and in people's behavior. You will have plenty of opportunity for observing and learning from people as you develop relationships with them.

Observation or interpretation?

Observations should be mere statements of fact; they record what the observer sees, but they do not contain any explanation of or assign any meaning to what is observed. As such, they do not - or at least should not - involve any interpretation.

Interpretations assign meaning to ("interpret") the facts; they involve conclusions, judgments. These interpretations inevitably come from the observer's experience of what the observed phenomena means in his or her culture. But if the person doing the behavior is from another culture, then that behavior may very well have a different meaning - with the result that the meaning assigned by the observer may be very different from the meaning intended (assigned by) the doer.

It is natural when observing a situation to interpret what you are seeing - and to come to a hasty conclusion about the motivation of the people involved. Because in our own culture we are able to base these conclusions on things we know about the typical ways people behave and what that behavior probably means. However, we need to be careful in another culture to actively practice *not* coming to quick conclusions and to keep an open mind about what is really going on.

We do have to interpret or make sense of the things we see and hear and we do have to decide what they mean - that is a normal function of daily life. So you should interpret what's going on around you, but you should know that when you interpret across cultures, you may sometimes be wrong. You can't be so sure of your interpretations - at least not until you understand the host culture better.

We will look at some examples of observation, as opposed to interpretation. In the following table you will find some pairs of statements. In each case, one of the statements is an observation, (a mere description of the facts or behavior you are witnessing), and the other is an interpretation, (your explanation or opinion of what those facts or that behavior means).

Observation	Interpretation
That man is talking quite loud.	That man is very angry.
That family dresses very well when going to town.	That family is wealthy.
That woman always wears a veil when she goes out in public.	That woman is quite conservative.
That woman never makes eye contact when she speaks to me.	That woman is cold and reserved.
That man never contradicts his boss in public.	That man is afraid of his boss.

BECOMING A COMMUNICATOR 1

She never speaks up in meetings.	She doesn't have strong opinions.
That worker never does anything until he is told.	That worker is lazy.
She said yes when the real answer to my question was no.	She lied to me.
They never show affection in public.	Their marriage isn't going well.
He yelled into his phone and used short, pointed sentences.	He's very aggressive/angry.

Here are some statements about the scene in the photo above. Sort the statements into two lists - observations and interpretations (answers are at the end of this tutorial).

- The women are standing in a group looking at something.
- One of the women's children is sitting nearby.
- The man is annoyed and wants me to go away.
- The walls are made of mud-brick.
- The man is interested in me taking a photo.
- The man is drinking a coke.

- The people are standing outside their home compound.
- The women are waiting for something to happen.
- The little boy on his own is bored.
- All women must cover their heads and wear long trousers.
- The house roof and wall is damaged.
- There are ladders going up to the roofs of the buildings.
- The women are wearing brightly coloured clothing.

❓ DISCUSSION POINTS

1. Below are some statements and quotes about listening - not just listening to learn, but listening as an important part of *relating* to other people - do you agree with these statements and why?

- Listening is the communication skill most crucial to success.
- Listening to gain information may be less important than listening to improve relationships.
- Listening is the skill that can make or break a relationship.
- We humans are relational individuals and it is sometimes as important to understand the person as what the person is saying.
- "Listening is as powerful a means of communication and influence as to talk well." John Marshall
- "I like to listen. I have learned a great deal from listening carefully. Most people never listen." Ernest Hemingway
- "If we were supposed to talk more than we listen, we would have been given two mouths and one ear." Mark Twain
- "What a shame, what folly, to give advice before listening to the facts!" King Solomon (Proverbs 18:13 NLT)

BECOMING A COMMUNICATOR 1

 **ACTIVITIES**

1. Practice active listening in your conversations this week. Make any observations about the way you normally listen and how easy or difficult it is to change those habits (if they needed changing). Also what did you notice about the way people listened to you?

2. Go and observe some kind of community activity or event that you have rarely or never taken part in before. This could be a sporting event, an entertainment event, an activity that others are doing, or a visit to a public place (it should be somewhere people are involved and where you can observe them closely). Take notes using the framework in the tutorial of the things you observed during the activity - the physical location, the human interaction, the communication, timelines and questions. Try to avoid taking an active part in things and affecting the behavior of people by your presence - your goal is to simply observe what is going on. Also note how you felt about the experience and how easy or difficult it was.

ANSWERS

Observations from the photo-
- The women are standing in a group looking at something.
- The walls are made of mud brick.
- The man is drinking a coke.
- The house roof and wall is damaged.
- There are ladders going up to the roofs of the buildings.
- The women are wearing brightly colored clothing.

Interpretations from the photo -
- One of the women's children is sitting nearby.
- The man is annoyed and wants me to go away.
- The man is interested in me taking a photo.
- The people are standing outside their home compound.
- The women are waiting for something to happen.
- The little boy on his own is bored.
- All women must cover their heads and wear long trousers.

4.19 Becoming a communicator 2

OBJECTIVES OF THIS TUTORIAL

This tutorial further discusses the concept that communication involves the whole person - that it is not just what we *say*, but who we *are*. Learning to communicate is not just learning language and culture, but involves an inward change so that we become suitable vessels of the mysteries of God and servants of Christ in a new setting.

Introduction

Effective cross-cultural learning is a process of *becoming someone who we currently are not* in order to be useful servants of the Lord in a new context. We have touched on some areas already where you may have been confronted by the fact that in order for you to be an effective cross-cultural learner, there may be a need for some personal changes - changes of habit, changes of automatic behavior or changes in thinking. It may involve becoming a better listener, a more indirect communicator or a better observer. It will involve stepping out of your 'comfort zone' at some point.

This kind of change requires a *willingness to change*. We are probably comfortable with who we already are, but for the sake of somebody or something else we are willing to go through the discomfort of personal change. Change is never an easy decision to make or a simple process to go through. It is helpful to think about *why* we should be willing to go through that process of change, and to understand what will motivate us along the way.

So some things about you as a person will need to change, but it is also important to remember to value the gifts that the Lord has given *you* - your personality, your experience, your background, your likes and dislikes, your skills - who you are in your uniqueness. Because being the person that God has uniquely prepared for the work He has given us is the best way to provide access to His message to the people we come in contact with.

Culture and language learning requires a process of deep change in our lives - the journey of becoming relevant and useful instruments in God's hands in a new context, and it is also a personal journey, one in which we will need to be wholly involved.

Examples from God's Word

Culture and language learning is primarily a time of learning and of gradually coming to a point of *knowing and understanding* the language and culture of the people. But the greater test will be going beyond knowing and understanding to *becoming* and *being*; becoming and being someone that you are not now; changing some things about yourself for the purpose of reaching the people God loves. Christ Himself is the foremost example of this and is a pattern for us.

Let's think of the example of our Lord Jesus Christ: through His incarnation, He so identified Himself with man, that it was later said of Him that He could actually "...*sympathize with our weaknesses...*"! He became a man, He gave up all the privileges associated with His higher status, and took on the nature and characteristics of humans.

Think about the life of the Lord in more detail, and how He actually lived among people:

- How did Christ relate to those among whom He lived?
- How did He love them?
- Which culture was He acculturated into?
- What kind of food did He eat?
- How did He dress?
- How did He travel?
- Was He part of the community?
- Where did He live?
- How removed was He from the normal life of the society?
- Did He escape? How? What for?
- What kind of privacy did He have?
- How did He relate to leaders of different types?
- How did He respond to the philosophies and worldview of others?
- How did He communicate?
- What language?
- What body language?
- Did He know the culture? As an insider?

Jesus came to initiate change and rebirth, so He did not become like us in *every* way.

His life exhibited a perfect balance of Grace and Truth - He made every effort to become like us in every way He could, but that did not stop Him from confronting the things He needed to, in order to bring Truth.

In 1 Corinthians 9, Paul gives a description of his own willingness to give up his rights in order to bring people to Christ:

> [19] *Even though I am a free man with no master, I have become a slave to all people to bring many to Christ.* [20] *When I was with the Jews, I lived like a Jew to bring the Jews to Christ. When I was with those who follow the Jewish law, I too lived under that law. Even though I am not subject to the law, I did this so I could bring to Christ those who are under the law.* [21] *When I am with the Gentiles who do not follow the Jewish law, I too live apart from that law so I can bring them to Christ. But I do not ignore the law of God; I obey the law of Christ.* [22] *When I am with those who are weak, I share their weakness, for I want to bring the weak to Christ. Yes, I try to find common ground with everyone, doing everything I can to save some.* [23] *I do everything to spread the Good News and share in its blessings.*

A lifestyle, not a series of tasks

As we have said, culture and language learning is much more than learning how to say something, we are actually learning how to *be* something. We could also say that effective cross-cultural learning is more a *lifestyle* that we grow into, than a check-list that we accomplish. It is a process of becoming a relevant participant and communicator in a new context.

There are certain activities and ways of living that will help you to grow and learn, and you will need to be pro-active in including those and keeping them balanced with other activities in your new setting. Here are some of the most important aspects that should be included in a healthy *lifestyle* of learning during the time of culture and language acquisition:

Spend time with people

Continually evaluate your schedule and activities to see if you are pursuing people rather than avoiding them:

- Find ways to be involved in regular activities in the community that local people also do regularly.
- Join a sporting group or activity where you are regularly with a group of people and the focus is on something other than you.
- Take a class at a college or university level in a topic that interests you.
- Do part-time volunteer work in an old-people's home, hospital, school, orphanage

- where you will regularly be with the same group of people.
- Have goals of meeting a certain number of new people each week, specific and measurable goals.
- Maintain existing relationships and evaluate how they are developing.
- Note when local people visit and meet to talk and try to join them.

Listen to people talk

This will happen naturally if you are spending time with people. The most effective way to boost your learning is to expose yourself to massive comprehensible input. That is, expose yourself to massive doses of speech (and perhaps writing) that you can understand, while gradually increasing the difficulty level.

Talk to people

This will also begin to happen naturally if you are spending time with people. You have to practice if you want to continue to learn, so you need to engage in extensive extemporaneous speaking. That is, engage in extensive two-way conversational interaction, and other speaking and writing activities.

Learn about people

Learn to know the people whose language you are learning. That is, learn all you can about their lives, experiences, and beliefs. Do this in and through the language as you spend time with them, and as you carefully observe them and ask questions. Have some broader learning goals as well, such as:

- gaining an appreciation and understanding of history, culture and community - both on a wider and a local level through individual contacts and relationships. In time this will help you to develop an overall understanding of cultural themes and worldviews.
- have an interest in national politics, entertainment, arts, religion, travel, and develop understandings about what is important to people.
- have an understanding of what friendship means in this culture, ideally through development of relationships personally.
- find out how the church (if it exists) looks and functions in this setting, and how it relates to other religious groups.

Get the most out of every situation

Use the principle that every situation has a multiple purpose - building deeper relationships as well as increasing linguistic ability and cultural understanding. Once you gain a degree of fluency through structured activities you will be more comfortable with unstructured social visiting as a means of getting conversational practice. You can use your formal language sessions to prepare for your general social visiting. For example, when you learn to discuss some topic in your language sessions, you can then make a point of discussing that same topic during informal social visits. You can even tell your friends, "This is what I have been learning to talk about with so-and-so", and then go on to talk about the topic with your friends.

If you have a job or study schedule in your new culture, it is particularly important to continue to prioritize language and culture learning activities as a part of your regular activities.

Balance your learning activities

One of the most difficult things to do when learning cross-culturally is to balance your time in various learning activities. So no matter what language program you end up following, you should personally make sure that your schedule includes all of these types of activities:

- *Formal language sessions* with someone who is providing comprehensible input and opportunities for extemporaneous speaking. During this time you have a safe environment to practice, ask questions and focus on particular things.

- *Personal study activities* in which you listen to recordings, read, write, and plan. Listening to a lot of recorded comprehensible material is very valuable as it prepares you for speaking with people. You can use this time to plan well for language sessions or to think about opportunities for social activities.

- *Social, work or community activities* in which you use the language, either in understanding messages, in uttering messages, or both. Purposefully identify situations - social/cultural - that you have not taken part in or do not know how to function in yet and learn how to do that. Participate in that situation, learn by observation what people say and what they do, evaluate what you need to learn, practice being in that situation until you know how to function. Your goal is to be able to function in this new context - to communicate to a level where people in this setting understand who you are and what you are saying to them at the deepest level. Also, make sure that you take time to just relax and enjoy other people's company, and for them to relax and get to know you.

Balance your family life

Finding God's direction for including your home and family life as an integral part of learning is a key to sustaining a healthy and enjoyable lifestyle of learning. This is possible, and can be a wonderful time as wives and husbands engage together in the challenge of becoming relevant and useful communicators and support each other in the learning process. Also, parents can find ways to help their children identify with their long-term goals, and help their children to be moving forward also in becoming more "insiders" in this new context. Children are a valuable part of the picture and should be included as much as possible in the deeper aspects of why you are there. Language and culture learning activities can be entertaining and satisfying for children as they grow and learn. Strong and healthy family relationships are an important way to honor God and communicate His character to those around you.

Who are we becoming?

We need to go beyond just knowing and understanding to *becoming* and *being*, in order to communicate fully what God wants us to. So who are we becoming?

Becoming...

>...a true friend
>
>...someone they want to be with
>
>...someone they trust
>
>...a part of their lives
>
>...someone they can talk to (because we *understand*)
>
>...someone they can listen to
>
>...someone they want to listen to
>
>...someone who can do things in the culture/language
>
>...someone who communicates at the deepest levels
>
>...someone who never stops growing

This process of becoming someone different is not simply a matter of learning language and culture so that you can accomplish a series of tasks...it's about undergoing inward change into a suitable vessel/steward of the mysteries of God - a servant of Christ.

❓ DISCUSSION POINTS

1. Someone has said that "cross-cultural learning for ministry is not merely learning how to act but becoming what we want them to become - modelling Christ in their culture. To help them to become, not like us, but uniquely like Christ."

Discuss this statement, do you agree with it, does it seem possible, is it too extreme, does it ignore other influences on their growth?

➡ ACTIVITIES

1. Following is an outline for a simple "ethnographic interview" that is used in a language school in Russia. It is used by people who are learning Russian and are already fairly fluent. Use the outline to interview someone you know very well - someone who comes from a different culture would be ideal. You can record their answers if you wish, but you do not have to submit the answers as part of the assignment.

Project "The Story of My Life"

Here are subjects you may ask about to learn the story of someone's life as an exercise in learning about the culture and the language at the same time. Be sure to tape the interview to listen to later for in depth language and culture learning. It is important to interview people from different age groups and social groups to get a better overview of the culture.

- a. Their country
- b. Their city or village
- c. Life in their country
- d. The different kinds of people in their country
- e. A typical day in their life
- f. An overview of their schooling (what their schools were like, etc.)
- g. A very happy day in their life (tell the story)
- h. A very sad day in their life (tell the story)
- i. Important events in their life
- j. Things they liked to do as a child

k. Things they like to do now in their free time
l. People who have had a significant influence in their life
m. Their hopes for the future
n. Stories they enjoyed as a child (or now)
o. Differences between their culture and yours
p. Their religion and how it is (or is not) important to them
q. What in their opinion is the noble life? (You'll have to translate the concept into their worldview.)
r. Major aspects of their religion (if the person is religious)
s. Specific questions about specific aspects of their culture and religion (Get them to talk about things that are ultimately important to them and their community.)

2. Now imagine walking up to someone you only know slightly, and asking them the same set of questions. How would the interview situation change? How would you feel and how might they possibly feel? What does this show you about language, culture and relationships?

3. Look back again in the tutorial at the list of headings under the title: A lifestyle, not a series of tasks. Think about your current activities and engagement with people in your community, and brainstorm some ways you could put more of these into practice in your current situation.

4.20 Practical communication 1

OBJECTIVES OF THIS TUTORIAL

In this and the next tutorial, we will look at how people grow in their ability to communicate and what that growth actually looks like in real life and in practical terms. We will look at both *ability* and *activities* at each stage a learner goes through on their way to proficiency.

Introduction

As we have already discussed, cross-cultural learning is about much more than just language learning, it involves your whole person, and can even be described as a process of *becoming a different person* - becoming someone who can communicate with proficiency in a new context.

We looked at what our overall goals should be and why we would have those particular goals for learning, and as a result, our definition of proficiency might read something like this:

> *"Proficiency is the progressive acquisition of culture and language, such that, as a result of the acquisition process, the learner earns the perspective, privileges, and communicative ability of a people group insider: namely, that the learner shares, with that particular people group, the intimate trust and understanding based on the specific, uniquely held people group worldview - that which is distinguished by an integrated set of values, beliefs, and behaviors, both cultural and linguistic."*

So, in practical terms what does it actually look like to move toward, and eventually reach, that kind of proficiency?

In these two tutorials we are going to 'paint a picture' as much as possible, of what it looks like to move from being a new person in a context, and knowing very little, to being able to communicate fluently as a member of your new community. We are going to take a 'snapshot' of what communication and learning looks like at four different stages in the learning process. We will see, for a learner at each stage, what *abilities* they might have at that stage and what *activities* they might be involved in at that stage.

Basic... Progressing... Capable... Proficient...

As people progress through culture and language learning, we are able to assess when they reach certain levels of proficiency. This assessment is based on how they actually *function* and are able to *communicate* in real life situations - not just on the amount of language they know. The four levels of proficiency that people move through are; Basic, Progressing, Capable and Proficient.

For any language/culture learning situation, each level has recognisable characteristics - at certain levels people are able to do certain things with the language and in the culture - so we can assess when a learner has reached a particular level, or has moved beyond one level and on to the next.

The levels of proficiency are not dependent on how much time someone has been learning or what program they have been following to learn - the time it takes to reach a certain level of proficiency will vary, depending on the individual learner, on the difficulty of the language, or on other factors. Proficiency is based simply on their actual functional ability to communicate.

Learning is a gradual process that looks different for every person and situation, and some aspects can't be neatly divided into sections and measured in some kind of scientific way. Even though this is true, there are some similarities that have been identified in the way all people grow in their ability to communicate cross-culturally. For example, there are clearly identifiable steps or stages in the way people learn to use another *language*:

- they begin with simple words and phrases,
- then they begin to use those words and phrases to make sentences,
- then they start to learn to join those sentences into paragraphs,
- and finally they are able to speak using extended discourse by linking the paragraphs together.

These identifiable characteristics of learners at different levels are evident in other areas as well - in cultural understanding, social interaction and cultural adaptation, to name a few.

We could represent this growth in proficiency as an upside-down cone (see the following diagram), with the pointed end at the most basic level, and gradually opening out toward the top where people are described as proficient communicators.

Beginning at the bottom of the cone, learners are 'brand new' in the situation and have little ability to communicate or participate. As they learn, they will grow in proficiency - increasing and broadening in their ability - toward the top of the pyramid where they will be proficient communicators and participators in their new community.

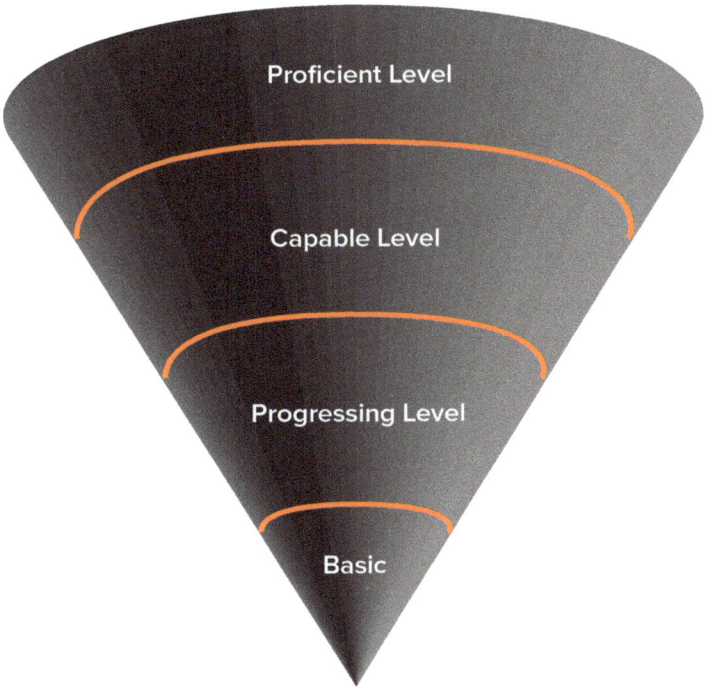

Proficiency includes areas such as language ability, pronunciation, naturalness, appropriateness, social proficiency, relating and socialization, and the learner's adjustment and adaptation.

Now and in the next tutorial, we will look at each of these four progressive levels of ability in more detail. As you read the descriptions of each level, imagine the lines on the cone, gradually climbing upward and moving outward in all areas of proficiency.

Basic level

At the beginning of Basic level, a learner will be able to respond to or speak a few isolated words – those borrowed from English, or commonly used, like *gracias, ciao,* etc. A learner at Basic level might describe themselves like this:

> *I can say "hello" and "goodbye."*
>
> *I can count to ten.*
>
> *I can use courtesy words such as "Thank you" and "Excuse me."*
>
> *I know a handful of words.*
>
> *I am eager to begin learning my target language.*
>
> *I have set some goals for my language learning.*

Still in Basic level, but a little further along in learning - perhaps after a month or so - they will be able to recognise and express very simple needs in polite language. They will mostly use memorized words and phrases and be able to say short phrases if given time to think about what they want to say. They might be able to recite a nursery rhyme or sing a simple song. They will recognise that they speak in a heavy accent with many errors and confuse sounds that are similar, and that their speech is difficult to understand, even to teachers used to working with beginning language students. They might describe themselves like this:

I can respond to simple commands such as "Stand up" and "Come here."

I can greet people and take my leave correctly, such as "How are you?" and "I must go."

I can ask basic questions, using who, what, when, and where.

I can make simple statements and commands such as "It's hot" and "Turn on the light."

I can make simple requests and appropriate thank yous.

I can use at least fifty words in appropriate contexts.

I can sing one verse of a folk song or popular sing-along tune.

I have to work hard to make many of the new sounds, and I often have to pause to find words that express my thoughts.

I frequently use circumlocution, that is, I choose words close to my intended meaning because I don't know the correct word I want. For example, I say "my father's brother's daughter" instead of "cousin."

I find it difficult to catch even words I know, when they are mixed with normal speech by my instructors.

People often ask me to repeat myself; some don't seem to realize I am speaking their language.

Toward the end of Basic level, after a few more months of learning, they will be able to ask questions and make simple statements based on memorized sentences, and understand conversation fragments and simple commands. They will be able to deal with simple topics of daily need though they speak mostly in short, direct sentences. They can say some longer phrases and sentences if given time to think about them first. Though they still make frequent errors in pronunciation and word use, and frequently ask speakers to slow down or repeat, they can communicate with close acquaintances (e.g., host family or co-workers) and behave considerately in dealing with host country people. They are able to correctly understand some non-verbal cues. They might describe their ability like this:

I can initiate and close conversations appropriately.

I understand and can make simple statements or ask simple questions about family, age, address, weather, daily activities, time, date, and day of the week.

I understand some words when the context helps explain them, e.g., in a cafe, the marketplace.

My vocabulary includes names of basic concepts: days, months, numbers to 1-100, articles of clothing, body parts, and family relationships.

I can use at least one hundred nouns and verbs in appropriate contexts.

I still find it difficult to understand native speakers (in spite of my growing vocabulary).

I often have to repeat myself, particularly when I'm with new acquaintances or strangers.

I am beginning to know what's expected of me in simple social situations.

I am motivated to build relationships, communicate and act in culturally appropriate way, and have a genuine interest in getting to know people.

Progressing level

Perhaps six months to a year after starting to learn - depending on the complexity of the language and cultural context - a learner will be moving from Basic to Progressing level. At the beginning of Progressing level, a learner will be able to speak about familiar topics, ask and answer simple questions, initiate and respond to simple statements, and carry on face-to-face discussions. They will be able to discuss topics beyond basic survival, such as personal history and leisure time activities. Though they often speak incorrectly, by repeating, generally they are able to be understood by native speakers who regularly deal with foreigners. They are now frequently able to understand native speakers if they repeat or speak more slowly, and are able to pick out the main idea in a simple conversation. They might describe themselves like this:

I can handle more complex questions about myself, including marital status, nationality, occupation, and place of birth.

I can read a menu, discuss food items with fellow diners, ask the waitperson about some of the dishes, and order a meal from a restaurant menu.

I can discuss simple topics with friends and feel comfortable that I can understand and be understood.

I am beginning to get the gist of some conversations and feel comfortable.

After a little more time, their ability will have grown further - they will be able to participate in more complicated exchanges. They will be showing improvement in using correct basic grammar constructions. And they will be showing more understanding of some common cultural traditions and taboos. At this stage they might describe their ability like this:

> I can travel by public transportation, asking simple directions or help as needed.
>
> I can respond to simple directions from customs officials, policemen, or other officials.
>
> I can handle simple business at the post office, a bank, and the chemist.
>
> I'm beginning to speak more correctly; my subjects and verbs generally agree.
>
> I am starting to understand and usually can behave appropriately in interactions that involve men and women, children and adults, and employers and employees.

Toward the end of Progressing Level, a learner will be able to participate in conversations about most survival needs, limited social conventions, and other topics. They can get the gist of most conversations on familiar topics. Though they speak mostly in short, separate sentences, they show occasional bursts of spontaneity. They can use most question forms, basic tenses, pronouns, and verb inflections, though they still speak with many errors. They can be understood by native speakers used to speaking with foreigners. By repeating things, they can frequently be understood by the general public. In dealing with local people, they are able to get along in familiar survival situations and with native speakers accustomed to foreigners. They might describe themselves like this:

> I can introduce myself or someone else in some detail.
>
> I can buy my basic foodstuffs, rent a hotel room, and bargain when appropriate.
>
> I can talk about favorite pastimes or sports.
>
> I can give and understand directions on how to get to places like the post office, a restaurant, or a local tourist attraction.
>
> I can deal with and explain unexpected problems, such as losing my traveler's checks or expiration of my visa.
>
> I can carry on more complicated conversations with native speakers who are used to dealing with foreigners.
>
> I find myself thinking some words and sentences in my new language and offering them spontaneously.

? DISCUSSION POINTS

1. What do you think will be some of the major motivations for you to keep going each day as you face the challenge of culture and language learning?

2. What do you think are some of the challenges you might face as you begin cross-cultural learning?

4.21 Practical communication 2

OBJECTIVES OF THIS TUTORIAL

In the last tutorial and this one, we will look at how people grow in their ability to communicate - what that growth actually looks like in real life and in practical terms. We will look at both *ability* and *activities* at each stage a learner goes through on their way to proficiency.

Introduction

In this second Practical Communication tutorial, we will continue to focus on the levels of proficiency. In the last tutorial we looked at the Basic and Progressing levels - in this one we will look at the Capable and Proficient levels. At the end the focus will be on the activities that learners at different levels will benefit from.

Capable level

Anywhere between a year or two years from starting to learn - or perhaps longer depending on the language and context - a learner will be somewhere in Capable Level. At this level, they are able to participate freely in most casual and some work conversations. They are able to give simple directions or explanations at work, and are able to talk about past and future events. With minimal requests for repetition, they can get the gist of normal conversation by native speakers speaking at an advanced language level. Their vocabulary is good enough to speak simply with only a few circumlocutions and they can speak extemporaneously and at an advanced language level on many topics. Though their accent is clearly that of a learner, they can generally be understood. They will have an expanding network of genuine/close relationships, hopefully with love and respect shown and understood. They will show appreciation, acceptance of differences and be able to connect on an emotional level. This is how they might describe themselves:

> *I can describe my work in some detail and discuss with my co-workers most work-related tasks.*

> *I can talk comfortably about topics of general interest, such as local entertainment and current events.*

I can talk about things that happened in the past or might happen in the future.

I can take and give messages by telephone.

I can be understood by most native speakers, and I can follow normal conversations involving native speakers.

Many of my thoughts about daily activities are in my new language.

After some further learning, they will still be in Capable level, but will have made more progress and will be able to handle most work requirements and conversations on technical or work related topics of interest. They will be able to express facts, give instructions, describe, report, and talk about current, past, and future activities. Often they will be able to speak fluently and easily, though occasionally they will need to pause to think of a word, and will still make some grammatical errors. In dealing with native speakers, they can understand common rules of etiquette, taboos and sensitivities, and handle routine social situations when dealing with people accustomed to foreigners. They would describe their ability like this:

I can hire an employee, discuss qualifications, duties, hours, and pay.

I can instruct a co-worker on how to perform a common task.

I can give opinions and facts, and explain points of view.

I can talk with ease about my past, my current activities, and what I hope to do in the future.

I generally speak easily and fluently with only minor pauses.

I can make culturally acceptable requests, accept or refuse invitations, apologize, and offer and receive gifts.

Proficient level

At Proficient level, learners will be able to converse on most practical, social, and professional topics. They will be able to deal with unfamiliar topics, provide explanations, resolve problems, describe in detail, offer supported opinions, and hypothesize. They can also talk about simple abstract ideas. They rarely have to grope for a word, and their control of grammar is good and errors almost never seem to bother the local person listening. They are able to participate appropriately in most social and work situations, and are able to understand most non-verbal responses; they are even beginning to understand culture-related humor. They have an expanding network of social relationships, and some of these are characterized by trust, friendship and respect, because the learner has earned the right to speak. With some people there will be friendly, relaxed, natural interaction and understanding. They might describe themselves like this:

> *I can carry out most work assignments in the target language.*
>
> *I can handle routine social situations with ease.*
>
> *I can participate effectively in most general discussions involving native speakers.*
>
> *I can handle normal and extended telephone conversations.*
>
> *I can listen to a radio program, oral report, or speech and take accurate notes.*
>
> *I can deal with an unexpected problem or a social blunder.*
>
> *I can support my opinions in a discussion or argument.*
>
> *I am beginning to understand jokes and word-play.*
>
> *I seldom have to ask speakers to repeat or explain.*
>
> *I can speak at a normal rate of speed, without groping for words or trying to avoid complex grammatical structures.*
>
> *I understand most body language and use it appropriately myself.*

Learning activities change as proficiency increases

As we looked in more detail at proficiency at each level, you might have noticed something significant about it: proficiency is what you can *do*, not what you *know*.

Proficiency isn't just learning pieces of information, or acquiring knowledge, it is growing in your ability to function and operate - to communicate and interact. That is an important thing to note because it has an effect on the types of activities which will be the most profitable at each level in order for you to keep learning.

Imagine if you were doing a course where you were just acquiring knowledge and learning facts. You would start out by hearing or reading those facts and then committing them to memory, then maybe practicing them in some way - perhaps by drilling or listening to them. Then you would learn more facts, and so it would go until you knew all of the pieces of information the course set out to teach you. The way you learned as you moved through the course would not really change from level to level - you would be able to keep learning and memorizing facts in the same way right throughout the learning process. But, as we have seen, cross-cultural learning isn't just about knowing things, it is about doing things, and actually functioning and communicating in real life.

As your ability to do things increases and changes, you are actually able to get more out of learning by increasing the complexity and level of your learning activities. You might start out very simply by learning some words or phrases from one person in their home, but you wouldn't want to be doing that same exercise three years down the track

- hopefully by then you would be learning by taking part in complex conversations with different local friends and acquaintances.

Activities for each level

As your ability to *do* things increases, so the way you learn things must change as well. Let's look at how the type of learning activities changes as proficiency grows. In Module 6 we will look in detail at a program that takes you through these activities, but for now, just notice how the activities change as proficiency changes.

Learners at **Basic** level would benefit from activities like these:

- Relating to people in the common and familiar situations.
- Learning by listening and acting (listening comprehension).
- Learning by listening and acting with speaking - predictable speaking activities.
- Participant Observation - being in situations and observing what is going on.
- Listening to simple recorded material that they understand.

Learners at **Progressing** level would benefit from activities like these:

- Relating to people as they go through daily routine activities - making new friends and finding out about their normal activities.
- Participant Observation - being in situations, observing what is going on and speaking as they are able.
- Working with daily routines - listening to recorded material with a helper, learning new vocabulary, learning new cultural concepts and ideas.

Learners at **Capable level and higher** would benefit from activities like these:

- Relating through sharing life stories with people - talking about things that have happened to them and about their past life.
- Participant Observation - taking part in life with people, observing and speaking. Noticing what motivates people, what they think and feel.
- Sharing life stories - listening to recorded material from their conversations with people, learning new vocabulary, and new cultural concepts and ideas.
- Relating through lifeview conversations with people - talking about what people think and feel about a variety of subjects and topics.

DISCUSSION POINTS

1. Why do you think it has increasingly become a requirement for business people working in other countries to take some kind of language course before starting their assignment? What level would you recommend a person reach before being able to work successfully as a manager in a factory? Why?

2. Do you think it would be possible for a person to learn the Spanish language entirely from a software program in their home country, without having the opportunity to speak to native speakers? What kind of issues with communication do you think they would notice if they suddenly found themselves in Mexico?

ACTIVITIES

1. Imagine that you have just arrived in a small city somewhere in Asia, and your student visa requires you to do a language course at the local university. This required course is conducted in an office building near your apartment, your fellow students are a small group of other foreigners and your tutor is a professional language teacher. Classes are for two hours a day, four days per week and focus on grammar points and dialogues with some speaking practice. How might you seek to supplement this course, and why?

ACCESSTRUTH

Training Resources for Making Truth *Accessible*.

RESOURCES FOR

- Discipleship
- Evangelism
- Church Planting
- Language Learning
- Bible Translation
- Cross-cultural work

Equipping God's people to be more effective as they serve in cross-cultural contexts, either locally or globally.

www.ingramcontent.com/pod-product-compliance
Lightning Source LLC
Chambersburg PA
CBHW061928290426
44113CB00024B/2845